slow cook

COUNTRY COMFORT
POTLUCK
FAVORITES

Over 100 Popular Recipes from Church Suppers, Firehouse Dinners, and Community Fundraisers

MONICA MUSETTI-CARLIN
FOREWORD BY ROLAND A. IADANZA

Hatherleigh Press is committed to preserving and protecting the natural resources of the earth. Environmentally responsible and sustainable practices are embraced within the company's mission statement.

Visit us at www.hatherleighpress.com and register online for free offers, discounts, special events, and more.

Library of Congress Cataloging-in-Publication Data is available upon request.

ISBN: 978-1-57826-514-5

Cover and Interior Design by Carolyn Kasper

Printed in the United States

10 9 8 7 6 5 4 3 2 1

Contents

Foreword

When you say, "I am going to be involved in running a fundraiser," there are many different reactions and emotions that come into play. As a chef, I believe it is a time to be creative, incorporating signature items from your establishment that you enjoy preparing into dishes that are impressive to both the eyes and the palate. The key principle for me is execution of a quality item that can be prepared efficiently without losing creativity and flavor.

There exists a burning desire inside each one of us to participate in these types of outreach events; to share our time and talent in aid of a good cause. For the past 11 years, I have been on the Steering Committee for the Great Chefs® Event, benefiting The Morgan Center, a preschool for children with cancer in Long Island, New York. It is the only one of its kind in the country, and offers preschool age children with cancer the opportunity to learn and socialize in a safe environment.

My planning for this annual event starts the day after the previous event ends, with my first thought being, "How can we improve the event for the following year?" Our structured committee meetings begin after the New Year to start planning the event, which takes place at the end of March. I personally ask approximately 25 to 30 food service professionals, food vendors, culinary students, vineyards, and spirit distributors to participate, and every year I am totally overwhelmed by the response. At the conclusion of each year's event, nearly all of our participants say, "No need to ask us to attend next year, we will be here," which shows the true sense of heart in every one of our contributors and donors. This is one of the most fulfilling evenings I encounter as a chef, because of our efforts, preschool aged children suffering from a terrible disease have a place to learn and have fun.

Included in this book are some of the most interesting and delicious recipes from food service professionals, experienced in planning and catering for large-scale events. Cooking for a large group encompasses the culinary French term *mise en place*, a phrase which describes a constant state of readiness or putting in place. Things like simplicity in execution are needed; precooking and blanching ahead of time, all while maintaining quality; efficiency must be paramount when preparing a large quantity of food for a great number of people. Monica has brought you these ideas and techniques through her research, obtaining these recipes from the finest "foodies" and compiling them in her cookbooks.

When my friend Monica asked me to reveal the secrets of running a large fundraiser, it was an easy response: planning, communication, organization, teamwork, follow-up, and, above all else, good old-fashioned *hard work*. Each participant preparing food must be ready to serve 500 people in a two hour time frame. They must often rearrange their schedules, and supply all of the necessary ingredients, food, and portable cooking equipment—organization is key. You have to be ready to adapt at a moment's notice, whether for no-shows, late arrivals, power outages, or items forgotten or left behind. And yet, through teamwork and camaraderie, it always gets done. Over the years, I have had the pleasure of working with many participants in a variety of capacities, whether behind the line or from a consultative and sales role. Many of these individuals are people that I have known for over 30 years. Thanks to these factors, this becomes a family event for us; it can be just the same for any community event. It becomes for us a special evening of loyalty, fellowship, and fun, which continues to warm my heart.

My congratulations to Monica on this book, and for recognizing what it takes to participate in all the charity events that take place across the nation. And my thanks for her always keeping at the front of her mind the reason we do it: it is all about the community.

Roland A. Iadanza
RC Fine Foods,
Suffolk County Territory Manager
Long Island, NY

Note to the Reader

In this, my seventh book in the *Country Comfort Cookbook* series, I have included recipes from my own kitchen and those of my favorite restaurants, accomplished chefs, Internet bloggers, family, friends, and neighbors. This collection is meant not only to be shared at your dining room table, but at the tables and venues of groups of people who gather together to share in communal joy or hardship.

The large-scale catastrophes, tornados, earthquakes, and hurricanes that seem to have become ongoing occurrences, and which many of us have now experienced personally, have brought together groups of people like never before, to lend a helping hand to their neighbors. And the same people who help during these tragedies are often the same people who are running your Little Leagues, bake sales, and your community's holiday celebrations on a normal day.

Here in my home state of New York, I've had many friends lose their homes completely to Hurricane Sandy. Many of them are still homeless, with none of their treasured possessions left, nothing but the clothes and what little possessions they could carry when they evacuated due to the massive surge of water that washed away their lives. They continue to battle to rebuild.

Teams of community members set up shelters overnight. Food, clothing for adults who needed something to wear to work, for their kids who had to have school clothes, sneakers, jackets, blankets, cleaning supplies, and dry bins were given out to salvage what little was left. Money was disbursed from collections at churches, schools, and organizations like Chambers of Commerce and civic associations to keep affected families going. The spirit of goodness and giving rose to the surface, above all other issues. Ongoing fundraising efforts took on a new dimension, as people would need help longer than anyone had anticipated. And through it all, people came to a greater appreciation of the need for fundraising, and the incredible strength and compassion of the community.

The awareness of the need for sustainability continues to echo in the thoughts and actions of many, and is always uppermost in my thoughts. When compiling recipes, I couldn't help expanding my thinking from growing in your own garden, to shopping local, buying local produce, honey, and cheeses, and also preserving what is in your garden. The meats and fish you've dried as a hobby have now become valuable, almost necessary knowledge. In a pinch, you will want to have at-the-ready food stored, healthy enough to maintain your family's nutrition, as well as being able to share with others.

The "we can do it" spirit that is so prevalent in our country allows us to survive any adversity, and we can do it while helping others and having fun, too. The pride of knowing that you have created something delicious, just from a handful of herbs or fruit from your garden, and the joy of sharing it with others at your town's country fair, at dinner with your friends, or at the firehouse or school are what make it all worthwhile.

Introduction:
Passing On Traditions through Food

There are many types of traditions that get passed along from one generation to the next: family member to family member, community elders to the next generation, even traditions within towns, all thriving within states and reflecting regional pride within our United States. There are traditions celebrated annually that naturally follow the four seasons: ad hoc summer fairs and festivals, celebrating events that have long since lost their initial significance—the first oyster catch of the season, or when the honey bees' golden nectar is ready to be collected. We continue on in the tradition of those who came before us, as we still celebrate the fall harvest, providing us with the winter's store of fresh fruits and vegetables, as well as bushels of juicy grapes to turn into fragrant wines. It's easy to imagine how an abundant catch of salmon could turn into frenzied excitement. After setting aside all that he needs for his family, the fisherman sells off what he can't use to neighbors, to local merchants and restaurants, maybe to other towns on market day. Commerce erupts. Trade begins, and continues. The town recognizes prosperity and everyone celebrates the good fortune together. Musicians join in, as theatrical productions recount the dramatic fish tales, and foods are prepared featuring the main attraction, the salmon. Contests pop up, resulting in delicious soups and stews, dried and smoked variations on old salmon dishes, as everyone explores the many creative ways to celebrate. And then, at the end of the day, the leftovers are given to those less fortunate. Everybody celebrates the bountiful catch.

Year after year it happens again, and the once casual celebration ultimately becomes a full-scale festival with the whole town involved. A simple market day turns into a fair; this is the true spirit of the community at work.

Traditional celebrations can also follow holiday schedules, school semesters, baseball seasons, summer vacations, and all the sorts of things people do throughout the year. But along with all the fun comes the need for the resources to facilitate it. At its simplest

level, all that this means is that core of community spirit: people helping people. On a small scale, this can be one neighbor to another,
sharing a potluck, or, in a much larger way, it can mean involving
whole communities, like the three day Summerfest in my hometown
of Sayville, New York, spotlighting the absolute best we have to offer.
Events like these have it all: antique car shows, food demonstrations
by local restaurants, art shows, craft vendors, artisanal foods, live music and theater, a carnival with rides, while all the proceeds go to the
town's community outreach programs, business initiatives, and local
charities.

Events like these always include fantastic food, delivered straight
from the heart and the proverbial "heartland," centered on the spirit
of community. It doesn't matter if it is a potluck shared at a church
supper, where 80-year-old aunties and grandmas whip up family favorites, whispering secret ingredients into an anxiously awaiting ear;
or, a big-city firehouse, where a daily meal is prepared by a broth-
erhood/sisterhood of heroes, all while working 12-hour shifts, when
they can be called upon at a moment's notice to gear up and fight a
blazing inferno before food ever touches their plates.

The recipes gathered here are from church suppers, firehouse
dinners, community potlucks, fundraisers, fairs, and festivals, all highlighting local game, seafood, wines, fruit, cheeses, honey, and vegetables. Each state in our great nation has its own regional specialties
that are celebrated annually at fairs, carnivals, festivals, and house
and garden tours, and from local pie contests to Chowderfests and
chili cook-offs, to boutique barbecues and more.

All of these recipes make use of unique ingredients, combined
in exciting ways that I've learned from the experts, to make delicious
stocks, sauces, rubs, infusions, brines, and marinades. They include
specialties prepared from a successful opening of hunting season
and the beginning of the harvest to celebrating the expansion of a
town and the changing seasons. Discover how to plan for a large
community event, and how to mount your own fundraiser or potluck. Learn to cook for five or five hundred. Included as well are tips
and advice on how to make your own sausage, dry your own garden
crops, dry your own herbs, and can your own fruit.

Take a stroll along Main Street, USA; experience the events I've
had the pleasure of attending over the years. As in all the *Country*

Comfort cookbooks, recipes will use sustainable, locally accessible products and ingredients wherever possible; fresh over frozen, frozen over canned, and canned only if necessary. Remember: the less processing your food goes through, the more nutrition it retains. Also, some foods in this collection are meant to be eaten only on special occasions, and are not part of any weekly diet; you will find several rich desserts and meats, but so long as you remember that moderation is key, especially when using salt, fat and sugar, your dishes will be a success.

The spirit of community, passed on from generation to generation, is embodied in this compilation of recipes and the stories surrounding them. As is the case with all things in life, you will find some of the recipes to be very difficult, while some will seem extremely simple. Choose your courses carefully and customize them to suit your taste. Be creative, be daring, and always keep in mind that you should enjoy what you have as well as sharing and giving back to your community.

Planning a Fundraiser

Let's start at the very beginning. Whether it is an individual, an organization, or a whole town, you need to first **establish your cause**. Why are you raising funds? It can be for anything from new playground equipment to a neighborhood cleanup, from renovating an historic church to planting a community garden.

What kind of fundraiser will it be? A one-night dinner dance, a casino night, a sampling of local wines and cuisine, a street fair and art show, a weekend seafood festival? Will you incorporate a raffle, a silent or Chinese auction, a grand prize giveaway (taking several months to sell tickets)?

Once you decide, **choose your date**. Determine whether you need a **permit** from your town. Often, food vendors will need a permit to conduct business, and sometimes an off-site permit is required when a restaurant serves outside of its dining establishment.

Choose your theme. Will it coincide with the holidays, or the annual hunting, fishing, or harvest season? Will it be in winter, spring, summer, or fall? The time of year will determine if it is an inside or an outside venue. Should you hold it at the firehouse or the fairgrounds, at the high school or the football field? Regardless of your theme, **decorate appropriately**. Flowers, candles, fine linens, silver, and stemware will do well at a sit-down dinner, whereas a barn dance may serve barbecue on paper plates and "moonshine" in a Mason jar.

Next, if you don't already have a group of **like-minded individuals** (such as the PTA, the volunteer firefighters, or your local chapter of the Pilot Club, Kiwanis Club, Knights of Columbus, or similar organizations), you will need to organize a group of volunteers who believe in your cause. The old phrase "many hands make light work" has never been truer: the more volunteers, the more helpers you have and the more monies can be raised.

Form a fundraising committee to **determine what your goals are** from the pool of individuals and groups who believe in your cause. Once that is done, you are ready to **organize subcommittees**. First draw upon family and friends, then neighbors, ultimately branching out to other organizations (like those mentioned above), plus school clubs, athletic teams, Chambers of Commerce, civic associations, and churches.

Your subcommittees will work together, coordinating efforts to fulfill your goals. **Set just how much money you will try to raise**. Plan on how many people the venue will hold. Depending on the theme, **what kind of food will be served**? Is it an apple harvest festival? Have a pie contest. A chili cook-off makes for a fitting Mexican theme, while a golf tournament, offering picnic lunches or an end of play cocktail party and dinner, lets you keep the event's momentum while you **choose a local person of note to honor**, whose name may bring in even more donations for your cause. If several restaurants are donating food, be sure to **coordinate who is sending what dishes**. You don't want five penne a la vodkas and several baked zitis (unless you are having a spaghetti dinner)! You'll want an assortment of dishes to spotlight the restaurants being represented.

Designate volunteers to handle every aspect of the event, from start to finish. **Create a timeline**. You will need committees to **identify and secure donations** of food and beverages, raffle/auction prizes, money, etc. The more that is donated, the less of the money raised will have to go to expenses, and the more your cause will benefit.

You will need **on-site helpers** to set up, and either sell or serve food and beverages, sell raffles and distribute prizes, or just handle logistics, like where the speeches and announcements will be made, or providing technical support for electrical needs like lighting or a sound system, security, housekeeping, and cleanup. All volunteers need to be instructed as to the appropriate way to fulfill their duties. If you are using teens, be sure they have an adult to report to and supervise them. Have a **drop-off and pick-up plan** with their parents, in addition to a **sign-in and sign-out sheet** for all volunteers. It's also nice to have **name tags** or matching T-shirts, to help the volunteers stand out from the guests.

Determine if you will be having **entertainment**. There may be a fee involved, so find out what it is. You will also find that most local school bands, choruses, theater companies, or dance studios appreciate the opportunity to showcase their talent, and will offer up their performers in exchange for the free publicity and the exposure your event will afford. Make certain whoever your voluntary entertainment is, they have a treat awaiting them at the end of their performance.

Securing **publicity** is important for drawing attention to your fundraiser. Ask your local radio station if they have public service announcement air time you'd qualify for. Cable TV stations may have electronic bulletin boards where local events can be posted. Send press releases to your local weekly or daily newspapers, asking to be included in their community calendars. Many times, a press release will get picked up and become either a pre- or post-story about your event. A pre-story is more desirable, because it has the potential to make more people aware of your fundraiser, whereas a post-story gives you the opportunity to show photographs of your event, building interest for next year. Look for particular aspects of your fundraiser that are newsworthy when writing your press release. If the fundraiser will be featuring specialty baked goods, it's not a bad idea to boost your chance for a story by sending choice samples to the editor. Social media like Facebook and Twitter are also vehicles to spread the word, as are direct mail postcards and good old-fashioned fliers distributed at schools and churches. If you have a budget for **advertising**, take out an ad at least a week before. If your event involves a sign-up for something like a house-tour fundraiser and space is limited, place your advertising a month prior, allowing time for anything to be mailed back and tallied.

A special written **thank you** to all vendors, venues, and volunteers who participated is always a nice idea; either a letter of recognition for a portfolio or something that can be framed and hung in the restaurant is appreciated. Inclusion in any publicity or advertising is also a great way to thank everyone.

After all the attendees have eaten (depending on the venue), food should be offered to your volunteers. If there is an abundance of leftover food, have a plan in place to package and deliver it to your local food pantry or shelter. It will be greatly appreciated.

Lastly, **present your check** to the institution, person, or organization that inspired you to have your fundraiser in the first place. Shortly thereafter, hold a committee meeting to discuss the positives and any negatives that can be improved upon. And then, finally, get ready to start it all over again for next year. Don't worry—the benefits always far outweigh the labor.

Fundraising Timeline

For a major fundraiser (such as the Morgan Center event), hoping to raise hundreds of thousands of dollars, preparation can take as long as an entire year. At the same time, it can take as little as one month for a school bake sale or car wash to get started. When planning for and organizing a fundraiser, it is vital to understand your working time frame and stick to your schedule, to make sure that everything goes off without any issues. While 2 to 3 months is the average amount of time needed for a successful fundraiser, the requirements are largely the same: it all comes down to the venue, the volunteers, the plan, and the people you plan to have attend.

One year prior: The very next work day following your event, assess how it went. Was there enough food? Was the bar fully stocked? Did all vendors show up? Did your team of volunteers and/or hired staff fulfill their required committments? Did you meet your fundraising goals? Make yourself a checklist and see to what you may need to apply extra attention next year.

Eleven months prior: "Thank you"s are the next most important order of business. Letters of gratitude need to be mailed to all of your volunteers, at every level. This includes the monetary sponsors, the venue management, and those who donated tangible gifts (like raffle items). I like to give a frameable award as well, noting the year and the name of the event, to hang in one's restaurant or office.

Ten months prior: Secure your current sponsors and the venue for next year's event. This will enable you to establish your budget and determine how much event development will be necessary. This is the time to apply for grants to offset costs, and to get commitment letters from sponsors. Make sure to have everything in writing so there are no problems at the time of your event. Seek out new sponsors as well, using the past success of your event as an opportunity to open new avenues of fundraising.

Nine months prior: Apply for any permits necessary, especially if your event is in a public park, a fairgrounds, or basically any outdoor venue. Establish a rain date. If doing an indoor event at a school, church, community center, etc., determine what fire codes you need permits for, as well as any health code permits you might need.

Eight months prior: Design your marketing materials. Even if your event is for the same charity as the previous year, change up the design to keep everything fresh and current. Don't simply drag out the old designs. If you want renewed interest for a previously successful event, you still need new materials that motivate people to join in at every level once again, whether sponsors or guests.

It's a nice idea to have a theme; plan to embellish your venue with theme-related decor, whether it be Mardi Gras in March, Cinco de Mayo in May, and so on. Coordinate where the decorations will be coming from; can you get them donated, or purchased for a discounted fee? Remember that your marketing materials will also need to reflect the theme you've chosen.

Seven months prior: Choose an honoree for your event. This will not only highlight a person who has been helpful to you throughout the life of your past events, but your honoree will bring their "following" with them to cheer them on. You could honor a local politician or community leader. This will benefit your event by adding a larger circle of guests, and will ultimately enable you to collect more funds for your designated charity or organization.

Six months prior: Send out your "Save the Date" postcards. You won't get responses from this mailing, but this will enable people to make a note on their social calendar and keep that date open for attendance at your event. It couldn't hurt to do an email blast encouraging a "Save the Date" as well, for those who are more prone to live their lives electronically. Utilize your Facebook page, your email list, etc. Cull through your sign-up sheet; if you don't have a sign-up sheet, make sure to put one out at this year's event, as it can be an invaluable resource for volunteers and guests. Update addresses and contact information so as to have the most up-to-date information for each potential guest.

Five months prior: Order your awards, plaques, etc. Strategize with your committee as to which media outlets to reach out, and update contact names and addresses. Put together your press kit to be handed out the evening of the event. The size and scope of the event will determine how many kits you will need. You may need anywhere from 10 to 100 kits. These kits should include the history and background of the event, photos, sponsors, and any other pertinent information you would like to appear in a feature article or TV spot. Establish your advertising plan, making sure that it includes a mix of print, email, and social media. Every event needs advertising. Write your press releases with an eye toward getting some free publicity, as well.

Four months prior: Connect with your volunteers at every level. Be sure everyone is on the same page. Confirm that the food has been ordered, the theme materials are in house, the raffle items are in the process of being collected, and any "day-of" clothing (such as T-shirts, aprons, chef's hats, and the like) have been ordered with a delivery date of 1 month prior to your event. Send out a checklist to all those involved via email as a reminder of what they have volunteered for, along with exactly what is expected of them.

Three months prior: Do a walkthrough at your venue to finalize logistics. Keep a folder with all the necessary permits, menus, volunteers names, and contact info. Send out your press releases to the media. Begin to place your advertising in any monthlies and secure your local TV spots if you have the budget for TV (or if your event warrants that kind of reach). Place yourself on the electronic community calendars that usually appear on community access cable stations. Finalize any music playlist, entertainment plan, or PowerPoint presentation you plan to have at your event.

Two months prior: Your preparations should now be in full swing; send out your invitations so they are received at least 1 month prior to your event. You should have already sent out your "Save the Dates," so this should be a more formal invitation, with full details of the event, along with an RSVP date. Levels of suggested monetary giving can be included in this invitation, along with suggestions as to how many guests will be attending. An open invitation that need not be RSVP'd to, like a reminder to attend a country fair or harvest festival, can be placed in your organization's newsletter, reminder postcard, or email blast, Facebook announcement, or in local community calendars.

You don't want to send out invitations too early, because there is too much room for error; the invitation could easily be set aside and forgotton. If you are advertising for attendees through local media outlets and require an RSVP to continue preparations, you may start advertising at this point. This will give any interested community members time to fill out any forms and return them to you so you will have them to add to your list 1 month prior.

Print your program for the evening; this should include the name of the event, sponsors, honorees, volunteers, and auction/raffle items.

One month prior: Expand your advertising to the general public. Ideally, you should begin advertising 1 to 3 weeks prior to the event. This will bring more people into your event, even those who have never been before. If an RSVP was necessary, you should have covered that with your mailed invitations and 2-month ads.

Secure your speakers, if any. Plan your podium program. Write the chairperson's speech. Write a script or program that those on the podium will need to follow. Arrange for the sound and lighting. Collect your raffle/auction items. Finalize food and drink. Pick up any printed clothing that the volunteers will be wearing. Secure your interviews with local media.

One to two weeks prior: Put up posters (if appropriate) in like-minded businesses or public places. Troubleshoot any problems with food, volunteers, venue, and entertainment: basically, review every detail and make sure you are ready.

One to three days prior: Do a final walkthrough of the venue to make sure everything—tables, lighting, food stations, linens, flowers, or theme items—are in place. One day prior, do a sound and lighting check. Have your media kits ready. Have your volunteers ready. Go over your final checklist to make sure you've left nothing out. Remind food and drink vendors of their timetables.

Day of (four hours prior): Dress appropriately to suit the venue. Do your final walkthrough, checking that all stations, staff, and volunteers are ready to go. Do a sound and lighting check for the podium speeches, as well as for any entertainment or PowerPoint presentation you may be having. Have scripts and media kits in place. Have your video or camera person available to document the event. Volunteers should be wearing appropriate clothing or a volunteer name tag. Have parking and outdoor signage arranged and in place.

Your reception station should be at the front door. There, guests will sign in with both name and contact information, receive seating assignment (if any), and/or have the opportunity to purchase any tickets they may need for raffles, food, or drink. Make sure to greet all media personally or have a designated person do so. Acknowledge any unanticipated dignitaries when you begin your podium program, as well as those you have already noted in your program. Thank everyone for coming. Follow your script.

Have fun, don't forget to eat, and don't get drunk! Have a good night's rest after your event, bank the monies raised, send photos and particular blurbs you'd especially like to appear in media outlets to editors and producers, and then…get ready for next year.

Planning a Community Potluck

If you are having a large group of people over for a potluck, the planning takes on a new dimension. Along with your appetizers and Entrées, serve a big salad with dressing and a variety of homemade breads and butter—and don't forget about dessert. Below are some additional tips for organizing a potluck:

- Start by determining the number of people coming to your potluck. Will it be all adults, or will there be children, as well?
- Assign each guest a dish to bring, specifying the course (for example, appetizer, Entrée, or dessert). Keep a list of each dish promised so you do not have duplicates of the same dish.
- Ask your guests to bring their covered dishes cooked in advance and ready to eat. For example, if someone brings a dish using chicken with bones, it should be cut into smaller serving sizes. Meats should be sliced into thin, easy-to-eat slices.
- The individual potluck dishes do not need to be enough to feed the entire party, because guests will sample a bit of each offering.
- If you know that any of your guests have a food allergy, you can either mention it to others who are bringing food or mark the offending dish once it has arrived for the safety of that particular guest.
- As the host/hostess, have ready all serving spoons, platters, bowls, and bread baskets in case they are needed. I find that having one or two hot plates on hand is also prudent.
- Before the potluck, inspect your dinnerware, glasses, and silverware for any chips.
- Be sure to have enough dinnerware to accommodate everyone.
- Arrange the buffet table with plates on one end, and the main dishes and accompaniments set out in the order that you would like your guests to take them (for example, salads first, then breads, and finally utensils and napkins). A long rectangular table is best, but an oblong or round table is just as good. Just be sure to have enough room for everybody's dish.

- Every guest should have a place to sit while they are eating and, ideally, a tabletop to set their plate on (for most potlucks, though, it is fine to stand and hold your plate). Folding chairs and occasional tables are a good idea.
- Appetizers should be set up in a separate area, such as on a coffee table or counters. This will help keep your main buffet table unencumbered and clean.
- There should be one table designated for desserts. I find most people will bring a dessert even if they have also brought an appetizer. Set out the coffee cups in advance: it not only looks pretty, but also saves you time at the end of the party to continue enjoying the company of your guests.
- Save room in the refrigerator for any desserts containing butter cream, cheesecakes, or carrot cakes with cream cheese icing.
- You should be responsible for providing the beverages, such as water, soft drinks, juices, and coffee. Also, be sure to have plenty of extra ice on hand.
- With regard to alcohol, have your guests BYOB, which means "Bring Your Own Beer" or "Bring Your Own Beverage." Or, if you prefer to provide the alcoholic beverage for the evening, you can make a signature cocktail for the get-together to serve as guests arrive.
- Arrange to have containers on hand for your guests to take home a sampling from the dishes that they particularly enjoyed.
- If you would like to be the ultimate host/hostess, have available blank recipe cards for someone who might like to exchange a recipe.

Part I:

BREAKFAST AND BRUNCH

Breakfast and Brunch

People helping people—that is what our country is all about. We have the knack for working hard at volunteering, all while having a good time. What enduring phrase does singer/songwriter Carole King sing out? "You've got to wake up every morning with a smile on your face and show the world all the love in your heart."

Sunday mornings for some may mean sleeping in, but for others it means, "When the going gets tough, the tough get going." Countless numbers of Americans, in hometowns across the nation, have fallen on hard times. Whether through the loss of a job, the loss of their home in a major storm, or a fatal illness in the family, these people don't have the luxury of sleeping in on a Sunday morning. That's when "the tough get going": a cheerful group of well wishers, perhaps the local chapter of the Kiwanis Club, who selflessly start out before the sun comes up to prepare a pancake breakfast for a couple hundred friends and neighbors, with proceeds going to a good cause. The main course might include Puff Pancakes with Berries (pg. 5) for everyone (with a side of sausage, smoked bacon, or Old-Fashioned Corned Beef Hash (pg. 13), or maybe toast with homemade Orange Marmalade (pg. 81).

Down the street at a local bistro, the morning menu has been set up to suit a brunch fundraiser for the Village Improvement Society, including smoked salmon, eggs benedict, Strawberry Crème Crepes (pg. 8), cream cheese French toast, and Turkey Breakfast Sausage (pg. 14) all washed down with a mimosa made with sparkling wine or a blend of freshly squeezed orange, mango, and pineapple juices (pg. 30) to create a zesty punch.

The causes—and the menus—can vary widely; perhaps the football team needs new jerseys, and the high school sports budget is spent, so how about a car wash, complete with homemade donuts (pg. 161), granola bars (pg. 23), and Banana Bread (pg. 28)?

There are so many different ways to lend a hand, to take a stand against apathy and step up to help, getting up for the occasion as the sun rises on another promising day. Sharing food with friends and having fun, all while throwing a 5K run to benefit the needy illustrates to the next generation that volunteering within their community not only helps strengthen their moral foundation, but serves as the building blocks for future endeavors.

Puff Pancakes with Berries

Serves 4

Every year, the fire department of Sayville, New York hosts the local chapter of the Kiwanis Club for a Sunday morning pancake breakfast. Burly volunteer firefighters cook side by side with the young recruits serving up endless trays of pancakes with maple syrup, crispy bacon, and gallons of orange juice and coffee. It is a family affair: neighbors both young and old turn out, and it is a chance to meet old friends and make new ones. The club donates the proceeds to various groups throughout the town, including scholarships for graduating seniors of Sayville High School.

4 tablespoons butter
¾ cup milk
3 large eggs
¾ cup flour

Pinch of salt
2 cups mixed berries (sliced strawberries, blueberries, raspberries)

Preheat oven to 450°F. Melt butter in a 10-inch ovenproof skillet. Blend milk and eggs. Add flour and salt, and then blend. Pour batter into the heated skillet, a tablespoon at a time, until batter is used up. Transfer skillet to the oven and bake until the pancakes puff and are golden. Transfer to four plates. Spoon berries on top and serve.

Quinoa Johnny Cakes

Serves 6

½ cup quínoa
1 tablespoon extra virgin olive oil (a little extra to grease griddle)

1 cup water
2 cups pancake batter
1 cup fresh raspberries

Syrup
1½ cups Vermont maple syrup
A pinch of cinnamon

1 pint fresh blueberries

Toast quinoa in oil using a saucepan. Add water and simmer lightly. Cover the saucepan for 10 to 12 minutes, or until all water is absorbed and the quinoa is tender. Turn off heat and let sit about 10 more minutes. Then, mix into pancake batter.

To make the syrup, heat the maple syrup and cinnamon with blueberries until they pop. Remove from heat. Grease griddle lightly with olive oil. Spoon on batter 2 tablespoons at a time, until all batter is used up. Serve with blueberry syrup and top with fresh raspberries.

Toasting your grain will result in a nutty flavor.

Venison Breakfast Sausage

Yields 12 servings

The opening of hunting season is a community event up in the Adirondacks of New York state. The Adirondacks can be some of the toughest terrain around, but the local hunt clubs are still joined by the city slickers and suburban hunters who leave home en masse, especially around Thanksgiving, to meet with friends and like-minded souls to hunt whitetail deer. Deer season starts at the end of September, and typically runs to the second week of December, with November usually being the most productive month. In a good year (and with an experienced guide) the hunt yields freezers full of venison, ready to be made into steaks, sausage, and stews.

5 pounds venison, fat trimmed, ground
1½ pounds pork, ground
3 tablespoons ground sage
1 tablespoon red pepper flakes

2 tablespoons fresh ginger (or 1 tablespoon ground ginger)
1 teaspoon fennel seeds
2 teaspoons kosher salt
1 tablespoon freshly ground black pepper

Grind the venison in a meat grinder, being careful to first trim off any visible fat. Add the pork and mix. Mix in sage, red pepper, ginger, fennel seeds, salt, and pepper. Refrigerate for at least 2 hours. Form into small patties and fry on medium heat, turning twice until firm and fully cooked (or until it reaches an internal temperature of 160°F).

Strawberry Crème Crepes

Yields about 20 crepes

Strawberry festivals are held all over Long Island and work to facilitate fundraising for all sorts of groups. Harbor Country Day School on the North Shore holds an annual weekend event offering strawberry-everything, plus games and entertainment. Proceeds go toward offering scholarships to attend the school, getting down to business while having fun.

1½ cups milk
3 eggs
2 tablespoons butter, melted
½ teaspoon lemon extract

1¼ cups flour
2 tablespoons sugar
Pinch of salt

Topping

½ cup sugar
2 tablespoons cornstarch
¾ cups water

1 tablespoon fresh lemon juice
4 cups fresh strawberries, sliced

Filling

1 cup heavy whipping cream
1 (8-ounce) package cream
  cheese, softened

2 cups confectioner's sugar
1 teaspoon vanilla extract

Combine milk, eggs, butter, and lemon extract. In another bowl combine flour, sugar, and salt and add to milk mixture. Mix together well. Refrigerate for 1 hour. Heat a lightly greased non-stick grill, medium heat. Spoon 2 tablespoons of batter onto the grill and thin out into a circle with the back of a spoon. Cook until the top looks dry; turn and cook several seconds longer. Remove and cool on a wire rack. Repeat until all batter is used up. (You may have to grease grill again).

Once cooled, stack the crepes with paper towels or round coffee filters in between each one. In a small saucepan, combine sugar and cornstarch; stir in water and lemon juice until completely smooth. Bring to a medium boil and cook stirring until thickened. Cool, then add strawberries and set aside.

In a small bowl, beat the cream until stiff peaks form; set aside. In a large bowl, beat the cream cheese, confectioner's sugar, and vanilla until nice and smooth; fold in the whipped cream. Spoon 2 tablespoons of filling, lining the center of the crepe; roll up. Top with strawberry topping.

Cream Cheese-Stuffed French Toast

Serves 12

12 (1-inch thick) slices of challah bread
8 ounces cream cheese, softened
6 tablespoons confectioner's sugar

2 cups milk
4 large eggs
1 teaspoon vanilla extract
6 ripe bananas
1 cup maple syrup

Cut a pocket in one end of each slice of bread. Beat together cream cheese and confectioner's sugar until completely smooth. Spoon about 1½ ounces of cream cheese filling all the way into each pocket.

Next beat together milk, eggs, and vanilla, before transfering to a large pie plate. Preheat a griddle or nonstick skillet over medium-high heat. Dip the bread, one piece at a time, into the milk-and-egg mixture as you would for regular French toast. Allow each side to soak very well. Place in heated pan. Cook about 3 to 5 minutes on one side, then flip and cook on the other side for about 1 to 2 minutes, or until golden on both sides. Repeat until all prepared bread is used up. Serve immediately with sliced bananas and maple syrup.

Breakfast Polenta with Chorizo Sausage

Serves 4

Nowadays, Cinco de Mayo is celebrated whether you are of Mexican descent or not. Fun, colorful, and festive, the theme has been used at countless fundraisers for a variety of different purposes. North Shore LIJ-Southside Hospital, in Bay Shore, New York (an organization I have worked with for years), holds one of their many fundraisers using a Cinco de Mayo theme. Surrounding restaurants, bakeries, breweries, and wineries all get together to celebrate and collect for a good cause. Whether it is expanding one of the hospital's wings to better facilitate the needs of the surrounding community or to purchase an important piece of technology for the hospital, this great community event draws attention not only to the gifting endeavor, but showcases all of the wonderful foods and treats the area has to offer!

1 pound yellow corn kernels, blanched 1 minute

1⅓ cups crumbled queso fresco cheese (about 6 ounces)

¼ cup red pepper, diced fine

½ cup fresh cilantro, chopped

3¼ cups water

1 cup polenta

1 pound fresh link chorizo sausage, casings removed

1 pound grape tomatoes (about 3½ cups)

1 jalapeño pepper, diced fine

Kosher salt, to taste

Freshly ground black pepper, to taste

Preheat oven to 425°F. Blanch corn and set aside. Mix cheese, red pepper, and cilantro. Mix 3¼ cups water, polenta, and corn in a 13 x 9 x 2-inch glass baking dish. Sprinkle with salt and pepper. Bake until all water is absorbed and polenta is tender (about 25 minutes).

Sauté chorizo until browned. Add grape tomatoes. Cover and simmer on medium heat for about 5 to 7 minutes. Uncover and break down the tomatoes, crushing them to create a sauce. Simmer until the sauce begins to thicken (about 10 minutes). Spoon the polenta onto plates and top with chorizo mixture, followed by the cheese mixture. Sprinkle jalapeño pepper and serve.

Polenta is yellow cornmeal and can be flavored to suit your dish, or just served with butter.

Old-Fashioned Corned Beef Hash

Serves 4 to 6

The age-old question: what to do with the leftover corned beef after Saint Patrick's Day? Once you have the taste for old-fashioned corned beef hash, it is never a problem again. Comfort food at its best, this dish is a real treat and goes well with any breakfast or brunch served after the day's parades and processions. The whole town benefits from the parades, as it attracts people from all over, benefiting local businesses on any Main Street, USA.

2 to 3 tablespoons unsalted butter

1 medium yellow onion, finely chopped

2 to 3 cups finely chopped, cooked corned beef

2 to 3 cups cooked potatoes, chopped into tiny cubes

Chopped fresh parsley, to taste

Salt and pepper, to taste

Heat butter. Add the onion and cook until translucent. Mix in the corned beef and potatoes. Spread out in a layer in the pan. Brown each side. Once browned, carefully stir in chopped parsley gently so as not to mash potatoes. Sprinkle with salt and freshly ground black pepper.

Turkey Breakfast Sausage

Liz Finnegan *(Islip, New York)*

Serves 4 to 6

An early morning mist hangs low over the gently sloping grounds of Monmouth Battlefield State Park in New Jersey. Continental and British reenactors have spent the night at the historic park, ready and waiting to begin the next day recreating one of the many significant battles of the Revolutionary War. More than 200 years later, little has changed, and the grounds are pristinely preserved by the park service.

The rising sun cuts through much of the fog, only to be replaced with the smoke of a plethora of campfires dotting the terrain, as the camp women cook the morning meals, while the men prepare for "battle," cleaning their muskets and filling paper cartridges with gun power. Musket balls are never used; this is only a reenactment. Reenacters travel all around the country, meeting up with other regiments to replay historical scenarios, all the while sharing their love of history with old and new friends. Together, they make a variety of meals, many from the period they are reenacting.

Just imagine: this sausage was once made from freshly caught wild turkey.

1½ teaspoon seasoned salt
1½ teaspoon freshly ground black pepper
1 clove fresh garlic, pressed, or ½ teaspoon garlic powder
1/16 teaspoon ground cloves
1/16 teaspoon hot red pepper flakes
1/16 teaspoon cayenne pepper
1 teaspoon fresh sage, chopped fine
¾ tablespoon brown sugar
1 teaspoon fennel seed
1 teaspoon fresh thyme, chopped fine
1 pound ground turkey
1 carrot, shredded, then diced
1 celery stalk, sliced thin, then diced
1 tablespoon extra virgin olive oil
2 tablespoons butter and extra virgin olive, for frying

Add spices and herbs one at a time to ground turkey and mix after each addition. Add in carrot and celery. Add in olive oil. Shape into patties and refrigerate covered overnight. Heat the olive oil and butter in a large skillet on medium heat. Place sausage patties into the hot skillet and cook until the middle is no longer pink. Drain off excess oil on paper towels.

Fruit Granola

Anthony Noberini *(Brooklyn, New York)*

Makes 5 cups

This granola recipe is quite simple and can be adapted to incorporate most dried fruits. It is great when served with yogurt and seasonal fresh fruits, like grapes and apples. It also makes a great homemade gift for any occasion. Be creative: try putting the granola into glass canning jars and top them with either an attractive label or the back of recycled brown paper bags, tied in place with raffia ribbon.

2 cups old-fashion rolled oats
1¼ cups sliced almonds
¾ cup sweetened flaked coconut
⅛ teaspoon salt
¼ cup vegetable oil

¼ cup honey
½ cup dried blueberries
½ cup dried cranberries
½ cup golden raisins or another dried fruit

Place oven rack to the middle position in your stove and preheat to 375°F. Line a shallow baking tray with foil, brushed with oil, or use parchment paper. Toss together oats, almonds, coconut, and salt in a large bowl. Whisk together oil and honey well in a separate large bowl, and then stir in the oat mixture until well coated. Spread mixture on the baking tray and bake, stirring occasionally until golden brown (25 to 30 minutes). Stir in all the dried fruit, and then cool completely in the tray on a rack.

Quinoa, Basil, Zucchini, and Sun-dried Tomato Frittata

Serves 5 to 6

⅔ cup quinoa

1 tablespoon extra virgin olive oil

2 zucchinis, grated

3 cloves garlic, minced

10 eggs, beaten

4 tablespoons fresh basil, chopped, divided

¼ cup sun-dried tomatoes

Cook quinoa according to package directions and set aside. Heat oil and add zucchini. Cook for about 4 minutes. Add garlic and continue cooking for about 4 more minutes. Add quinoa and cook, stirring constantly for approximately 2 minutes. Combine eggs, basil, and sun-dried tomatoes in a bowl, then add to the pan and mix with other ingredients. Cook until liquid is mostly absorbed and place in a 350°F oven and bake for 8 to 10 minutes or until all liquid is absorbed and eggs are firm.

Vegetarian's Delight Tempeh Hash

Liz Finnegan *(Islip, New York)*

Serves 4

Liz is a great cook who loves to host brunch at her home for friends and family, as well as those who share common community interests like history. Her husband Rob served as the town of Islip historian for many years. Being a vegetarian, she always makes certain to include tasty meatless dishes.
—*Monica*

1 yellow onion, diced
4 Yukon Gold potatoes, diced, boiled, drained well
1 package tempeh, cut into ½-inch cubes

3 tablespoons extra virgin olive oil
2 tablespoons soy sauce
½ teaspoon garlic powder
Sea salt, to taste

Sautee the onions, potatoes, and tempeh in olive oil and soy sauce. Mix in the garlic powder and salt. Serve on the buffet table.

"On the Run" Granola Bars

Joanne and Adam Gallagher

Yields 12 bars

> The Oakdale Chamber of Commerce in New York, of which I've served as president for many years, runs several fundraisers annually. Wherever possible, we share a portion of the proceeds with worthy causes throughout the community, while the rest is saved to offset the costs for such events as the Christmas tree lighting, Easter egg hunt, and especially our Firecracker 5K every Fourth of July. When the runners complete the course, there are only three things on their mind: their time, a drink of water, and eating something nourishing, like fresh oranges or (as a special treat) a granola bar to perk them up after expending so much energy.
> —*Monica*

2½ cups old-fashioned rolled oats
½ cup whole almonds, coarsely chopped
¼ cup unsalted butter, cut into pieces
⅓ cup honey
¼ cup packed light brown sugar

½ teaspoon vanilla extract
¼ teaspoon kosher salt
½ cup dried cranberries, coarsely chopped
6 tablespoons mini chocolate chips, divided
1 tablespoon vegetable oil

Heat oven to 350°F. Line bottom and sides of an 8-inch square pan with aluminum foil. Then lightly grease with oil. Place oats and almonds on a baking sheet and bake for 5 minutes. Stir and bake another 3 to 5 minutes to lightly toast. Transfer bowl and set aside.

Combine butter, honey, brown sugar, vanilla extract, and salt and cook, stirring occasionally until butter melts and the sugar completely dissolves.

Mix butter mixture into bowl with toasted oats and almonds. Let cool for about 5 minutes, then add cranberries and 4 tablespoons of the mini chocolate chips. Stir and transfer the entire mixture to your lined pan. Firmly press the mixture into the pan before sprinkling on the remaining chocolate chips, and gently press them into the top. Cover and refrigerate at least 2 hours.

Once chilled, remove from pan and peel away aluminum foil. Cut into 12 bars. These can be stored in an airtight container for up to 1 week, either at room temperature (which will yield a softer bar) or refrigerated (which results in a harder consistency).

These make great Christmas gifts at the office or in the kids' stockings. Just wrap in clear cellophane and tie with a festive ribbon.

Part II:

LUNCH

LUNCH

Lunch has many faces. It's the "on-the-go" meal, the midday pause when we know we should stop and take a breather, but so often either forget or ignore during the day's events. Too often we decide to "just wait until dinner," when we know that we tend to overeat, because we are starving.

Some days, you just cannot get away from your desk. Why not take a moment or two to enjoy a hot bowl of nourishing homemade soup? All it takes is a couple of minutes to heat in the office microwave, making your co-workers jealous as the aroma wafts down the hallway. Soon, you will find each person in turn coming to the kitchenette to join you. It makes for good morale to have a little down time together, even if it is just a quick conversation, sharing the new recipe for Sweet Potato Bisque (pg. 41) you've just learned from one of your neighbors at the last weekend potluck. You'll find that you have a more productive afternoon companywide if you reward yourself with a break and something delicious. Another benefit to taking the time to have lunch is that you have the opportunity to work off those calories; you know that you will be active (at least mentally, possibly physically) until your workday is over.

Lunch, with its "on-the-go" flexibility, allows you to have fun *and* raise funds, all at the same time. Working together to present the best the community has to offer allows you to show your pride in your hometown, as small businesses work together to attract potential guests at each destination, delighting them with haute cuisine and highlighting fresh local produce and cheeses. Proceeds of these tours and many others like it go toward continued promotional endeavors, keeping businesses and charitable organizations thriving, and enabling the beautiful and bountiful terrain of the area to remain intact.

Good works take many forms, and good people have many different personas. What you may see on the exterior may not be a good indication of what lies within. Take, for example, the annual "Toy Run," during which Harley Davidson owners from all across the country join forces and ride en masse to bring toys to children in orphanages and foundling homes. Tens, sometimes hundreds of leather-clad motorcycle enthusiasts, some with seemingly gruff countenances, exhibit hitherto unseen tenderness as they hand a less-fortunate child a special gift, picked just for them at holiday time. Afterward, often joined by family and friends, they'll convene at a local VFW hall and have an afternoon meal of a Brooklyn-Style Six-Foot Italian Hero (pg. 55) with Red Potato Salad with Bacon (pg. 60) together before the ride back home. Good food, good people, good vibrations.

Before your "get up and go" has "got up and went," take the time to see where *you* may be needed in your community. It is not only a good thing to do; it is a good feeling to be able to do something to help someone else. Have your lunch first; make sure you have the energy to give it your all, and bring along a friend or two! "Many hands make light work," so many hands can help to make someone's burden just a little lighter.

South Shore Crab Cakes

Maureen Denning, Snapper Inn *(Oakdale, New York)*

Yield 15 2-ounce crab cakes

Long Island towns are home to many of the historic mansions of the past: the Bourne Estate, Vanderbilt Mansion, Roosevelt's Meadow Croft, Bayard Cutting Arboretum, Sagtikos Manor, where George Washington passed through, just to name a few. Thanks to the ongoing interest of the surrounding communities, the dedicated work of tireless volunteers, and in some cases the towns they are housed in, these mansions have survived, and are either in the process or have already been restored (inside and out) to their former glory. Regaining their regal status in our nation's history, countless luncheons, tag sales, teas, and benefits contributed to the monies it took to keep these structures alive for the next generation to appreciate. An afternoon luncheon serving local seafood is just one of the ways of raising funds that go toward these important projects.

—*Monica*

1 pound crabmeat (lump)
1 red pepper, diced small
1 bunch chives
1 cup Japanese bread crumbs (panko)

1 tablespoon Old Bay®
¼ cup lemon juice
¾ cup mayonnaise
Tabasco®, to taste
Salt and pepper, to taste

Mix all ingredients together, except the crabmeat. Slowly fold the crabmeat into the mixture (to keep large chunks). Let sit 2 hours (refrigerated). Make into 2-ounce patties. Pan sear for 1 minute on each side. Bake in oven at 350°F for 5 minutes. Serve.

Fisherman's Catch Salmon Chowder

Serves 4

½ pound red potatoes, scrubbed, cut into ½-inch cubes, skin on

½ pound sliced bacon, cut crosswise into ¼-inch-wide strips

2 cups chopped scallions (from 2 bunches)

1 cup frozen corn, or 2 large ears broken into threes

1 tablespoon garlic, finely chopped

1 teaspoon fresh thyme, finely chopped

1 small bay leaf

½ cup red bell pepper, diced small

⅛ teaspoon dried hot red pepper flakes

3 cups whole milk

⅔ cup heavy cream

2 tablespoons cream sherry

1 (1½-pound) piece wild salmon fillet, cut into 1-inch pieces

½ teaspoon kosher salt

¼ teaspoon freshly ground black pepper

2 teaspoons fresh lemon juice

Cook potatoes until tender. Drain and set aside. Cook bacon until crisp, not burned. Drain grease on paper towels. Reserve 2 tablespoons bacon fat from pan and use it to cook scallions, corn, garlic, thyme, bay leaf, red bell pepper, and red pepper flakes (about 4 to 6 minutes). Add milk and cream and bring just to a boil. Add the sherry, stirring constantly until fully blended. Reduce heat to moderately low, then add potatoes, salmon, bacon, salt, and pepper and cook, occasionally stirring gently, until salmon is cooked and is beginning to break up into bite-size chunks (about 6 to 10 minutes). Add lemon juice, stirring to blend well, but careful not to break the salmon into too-small pieces. Add salt and pepper to taste. Discard bay leaf before serving.

Blue Point Oyster Stew

Mary Carlin *(East Meadow, New York)*

Serves 4 to 6

Chris Quartuccio, CEO of the Blue Island Oyster Company, has been farming the virtually extinct Blue Point oysters in a hatchery in their native waters in West Sayville. The effort has brought together community groups, historians, fishing fleets, and local government to help promote the project through lectures, fairs, fundraisers, and art shows spotlighting both the industry's history and future. This is my mother-in-law Mary's oyster stew, a dish which she only ever made in the months that had an "r" in them.

—Monica

---

1 pint oysters, shucked, liquor reserved

5 tablespoon butter

¼ cup flour

2 celery stalks, trimmed and minced

1 medium yellow onion, minced

1¾ cup milk

¼ cup cream

1 teaspoon hot sauce

½ cup parsley, minced

Sea salt and freshly ground black pepper, to taste

Strain the oyster juice into a bowl to remove any grit and reserve the juices. Rinse the oysters well under cold water and put them into a separate bowl. Melt the butter in a pot over medium heat. Add the flour and stir to make a roux. Cook for a few minutes, then stir in the celery and onions and cook for 2 to 3 minutes. Continue stirring, then add the bottled oyster juice and any liquor released from the oysters.

Add the milk and cream, continuously stirring. Add the hot sauce. Simmer for 15 minutes, careful not to let it boil. Add the oysters and cook for another 2 minutes. Garnish with parsley. Add salt and pepper to taste.

Quick Chicken Vegetable Soup

Kathleen Gallagher *(Oakdale, New York)*

Serves 4 to 6

> Soup suppers appear regularly at local churches: events where the community gets together to share a pot of piping-hot soup and good conversation with friends and neighbors. In my church, the kids not only serve, but also help make the soup. About twenty or so giant pots appear, and bowl after bowl is ladled out until you've had a chance to sample every one (that is, if you *can* sample every one). All the leftovers are then donated to local soup kitchens and food pantries for the needy.
>
> Almost everybody loves this chicken vegetable soup; it just seems to say "home" to people, even if just for one evening.
> —*Monica*

1 tablespoon butter
½ yellow onion, chopped
2 garlic cloves, minced
1 pound chicken breast, cut into 1-inch chunks
2 large carrots, chopped
3 celery stalks, chopped

1 cup fresh green beans, chopped into 1-inch pieces
4 sprigs fresh thyme
5 to 6 cups water, as needed to cover
1½ teaspoons salt
Salt and pepper, to taste

Sauté the onion, garlic, and chicken in the butter for about 5 minutes. Add the carrots, celery, green beans, thyme leaves, and enough water to just cover the vegetables (about 5 to 6 cups). Bring the water to a boil, then reduce heat and allow to simmer for 20 minutes.

Soft Pretzel Rolls

Harry Myers *(Lipan, Texas)*

Yields 13 rolls

> What is soup without a piece of bread to dunk into the broth? Harry does it again with this old-fashioned pretzel roll recipe.

1 cup warm water (105°F to 115°F)

¼ ounce (1 packet) active dry yeast (2¼ teaspoons)

Vegetable oil

2¾ cups bread flour, plus more for dusting your work surface

1 tablespoon sugar

1 teaspoon kosher salt, plus more for sprinkling

6 cups water

¼ cup baking soda

Place the warm water in the bowl of a standing mixer and sprinkle the yeast on top. Set aside to rest until the mixture bubbles (about 5 minutes). If the mixture does not bubble, either the liquid was not at the correct temperature or the yeast is old. Meanwhile, coat a large mixing bowl with a thin layer of vegetable oil and set aside.

Place the flour, sugar, and measured salt in a large bowl, whisk briefly to break up any lumps, and combine. Once the yeast is ready, fit the bowl on the mixer, attach a dough hook, and dump in the flour mixture. Mix on the lowest setting until the dough comes together, then increase to medium speed and mix until the dough is elastic and smooth (about 8 minutes).

Form the dough into a ball, place in the oiled mixing bowl, and turn the dough to coat in oil. Cover with a clean, damp dishtowel and let rest in a warm place until the dough doubles in size (about 30 to 35 minutes). Line a baking sheet with parchment paper, coat the paper with vegetable oil, and set aside.

Once the dough has risen, punch it down and knead it on a floured, dry surface just until it becomes smooth and springs back when poked (about 1 minute). Divide the dough into eight pieces and form into oblong rolls. Place the rolls on the baking sheet and cut four (2-inch) diagonal slashes across the top of each. Cover with a damp towel and let the dough rise in a warm place until almost doubled in volume (about 15 to 20 minutes). Meanwhile, heat the oven to 425°F and bring the 6 cups of water to a boil in a large saucepan over high heat.

Once the rolls have risen, stir the baking soda into the boiling water (the water will foam up slightly). Boil two or three rolls for 2 minutes per side. Using a slotted spoon, remove the rolls, drain, and place on the baking sheet, cut-side up. Sprinkle well with salt and repeat with the remaining rolls.

Once all the rolls are ready, place in the oven and bake until golden brown (about 10 to 12 minutes). Serve hot.

Seafood Chowder

Emily Elliot *(Brooklyn, New York)*

Serves 6

I served this at a party last summer, out in the Hamptons. Out east it's one fundraiser after another, with proceeds going to causes both local and national. One bowl of soup goes a long way!

When I worked as a recreational therapist at a nursing home, I belonged to a cooking group in which the ladies would share the recipes of their childhood. We'd make a lunch together and share a bowl of good cheer. It was an institutional community effort, sharing food like a family would. This is a recipe from those days, from a member of my group. We never actually made it at the nursing home, as lobster wasn't a readily available ingredient, but many of the residents so wanted to share their recipes with me so to ensure that they would be saved for a lifetime and passed down once they were gone. This one is for you, Emily.

—Monica

4 tablespoons unsalted butter

3 sprigs thyme

1 bay leaf

1 large yellow onion, finely chopped

1 pound potatoes, peeled and cut into cubes

1 cup half-and-half

1 cup heavy cream

4 cups water

1 pound haddock, cut up into bite size pieces

6 ounce bay scallops

4 ounce cooked lobster meat, chopped

1 (9¾-ounce) jar whole baby clams, in their liquid

Kosher salt and freshly ground black pepper, to taste

Heat butter in a 4-quart saucepan over medium-low heat. Add thyme, bay leaf, and onion; season with salt and pepper and cook, covered, stirring occasionally, until onion is soft.

Add potatoes, half-and-half, cream, 4 cups of water and simmer uncovered, stirring occasionally (about 15 minutes or until potatoes are fork tender). Add haddock and scallops and cook (about 5 minutes), stirring once. Add lobster and clams, and cook another 3 minutes more. Serve in blue and white bowls with oyster crackers.

Holiday Chestnut Soup

Emily Elliot *(Brooklyn, New York)*

Serves 12

> Hardly anyone cooks with chestnuts anymore. Those giant, brown beauties, when roasted, fill the air with an unmistakable fragrance during the holiday season, as Salvation Army Santas on street corners collecting money to enable less fortunate families to enjoy a Christmas dinner. Many of the holiday parties I attend also have an element of gift giving beyond that of just giving to each other. It is acceptable to ask one to bring a gift for a girl or boy, to give to the Boys and Girls Club of America or the Catholic Guardian Society, spreading the joy while passing round this delectable soup.
> —*Monica*

3 cups roasted bottled chestnuts, whole
2 cups yellow onion, chopped
¾ cup carrot, thinly sliced
1 tablespoon extra virgin olive oil
6 cups chicken stock
2 tablespoons cream sherry
½ teaspoon kosher salt
¼ teaspoon freshly ground multicolored pepper
⅓ cup heavy whipping cream
1½ teaspoons fresh thyme, minced
½ cup dried cranberries

Preheat oven to 400°F. Roast chestnuts on a pan for 15 minutes, then remove to a large bowl and cool to room temperature. Combine onion, carrot, and oil in pan; toss to coat vegetables. Bake at 400°F for 1 hour or until tender, stirring occasionally. Add to chestnuts; stir in stock and sherry. Pour half of stock mixture into a blender; blend until smooth.

Pour pureed mixture into a large soup pot. Repeat process with remaining stock mixture. Stir in salt and pepper. Simmer for 25 minutes. Beat cream until soft peaks form. Serve hot with a dollop of cream, a sprinkling of thyme, and a few cranberries.

To roast chestnuts in their shell, preheat oven to 425°F. On the flat side of each chestnut, cut an X deeply into the skin. Place on a baking pan and roast for about 30 to 40 minutes. Rotate chestnuts to cook evenly. Peel as soon as they are cool enough to handle, as they will be difficult to peel once fully cooled.

North Atlantic Salmon with Wilted Arugula, White Zinfandel Sauce, and Fried Capers

Chef Roland Iadanza *(Commack, New York)*

Serves 4

Chef Roland is much in demand in the food industry. He is an accomplished chef, Chowderfest judge, contributor to several books in my Country Comfort series, and one of the forces behind the ongoing fundraising efforts of the Morgan Center in Long Island.

—*Monica*

For the sauce:

6 tablespoons chopped shallots

2 ounces champagne vinegar

4 ounces white zinfandel

1 ounce lemon juice

2 ounces heavy cream

4 ounces sweet butter

Salt and pepper, to taste

Additional Ingredients

Vegetable oil, for sautéing

4 salmon fillets, 6 to 8 ounces each

Olive oil, for sautéing

3 tablespoons chopped shallots

½ pound arugula

4 ounces capers, deep-fried

Salt and pepper, to taste

Reduce shallots, champagne vinegar, white zinfandel, and lemon juice by a quarter in a stainless steel saucepan. Add cream and reduce by half until slightly thickened. Remove from heat and whisk in butter, a little at a time. Add salt and pepper to taste. Then strain through fine-mesh strainer. Hold for service.

Heat vegetable oil in sauté pan; add salt and pepper. Sear salmon skin-side up. Turn over and place in 500°F oven for 4 minutes until firm to the touch. Heat olive oil in sauce pan; add chopped shallots and sauté for 1 minute. Add arugula and toss until slightly wilted. Place in center of dinner plate. Place salmon on top of arugula. Ladle sauce around fish and garnish with fried capers.

Healthy Salad

Chef Ron Gelish, RandA Healthy Concept LLC *(Holbrook, New York)*

In an age of health consciousness, Chef Ron shows people how to cook in a healthy, timely, and energy-efficient manner. He travels to homes all over Long Island, Manhattan, and even Connecticut to cook and clean for parties of about two to eight people. Amazingly, his in-home cooking demonstrations are free, because his presentations are a means of advertising the Saladmaster® premium cooking ware he uses to prepare a meal that's healthy and oil free.

The key to the bold tastes of his healthy food is the cooking method and utensils. I met him at the annual Morgan Center Benefit, where he shared his recipes as one of the fifty chefs donating their time and expertise to raise enough money to account for a portion of the Center's operating expenses for much of the year.

—*Monica*

2 ounces reduced-fat or fat-free
   cheddar cheese
1 medium carrot
⅓ head green cabbage
¼ head red cabbage
½ zucchini
3 radishes

1 red apple
1 lemon, zest and juice
1 teaspoon sea salt
Lemon zest, to taste
Lemon juice, to taste
Sea salt, to taste

Shred cheese, carrot, cabbages, zucchini, radishes, and apple using a medium shredding setting. Place all ingredients in bowl. Serve with your choice of salad dressing.

Caramelized Onion Pasta Salad for a Crowd

Jaclyn L. Messina, Jac's Bakeshop and Bistro: Long Island's Completely Gluten Free Bakery *(Hicksville, New York)*

Yields 50 shooter cups (appetizer size in shot glass) or 18 to 22 full servings

On a cold winter's night, a fire let off a spark that ignited a dream in a celiac baker's heart. That dream became a vision; that vision inspired determination, before finally becoming a reality.

My name is Jaclyn Messina. I am the owner and executive baker at Jac's Bakeshop and Bistro in Hicksville, New York. Back in 2009 I was diagnosed with celiac disease, and then later in 2010 with an egg allergy as well. Being a professional baker already and a natural-born foodie, I had to find ways to prepare all the same foods I already loved, but now gluten free. After years of trial and error at my gluten free Bakeshop and Bistro, I have created a one-of-a-kind menu for the whole family to enjoy, gluten free or not: recipes that are extraordinarily scrumptious, safe, and affordable.

Roasted Garlic Dijon Vinaigrette

2 heads roasted garlic
2 cups extra virgin olive oil
½ cup stone-ground mustard
⅓ cup apple cider vinegar
¼ cup maple syrup
¼ cup honey

Pasta Salad

3 medium Vidalia onions, thinly sliced
1½ pounds center-cut bacon
3 pound gluten-free fusilli pasta (Ronzoni® preferably)
2 cups dried cranberries
2 cups crumbed goat cheese
3 cups toasted cashews
Salt and pepper, to taste
6 tablespoons butter
6 tablespoons oil
6 tablespoons sugar

Cut off top of garlic. Place in foil and drizzle with olive oil. Close foil, pinching at the top, and place in a preheated 375°F oven for 45 to 60 minutes until garlic is soft and golden. Remove from oven and let stand for 20 minutes. Remove from foil and squeeze garlic out into bowl. Add remaining dressing ingredients and whisk until combined. Salt and pepper to taste.

In a large frying pan, heat 6 tablespoons butter, 6 tablespoons oil, 6 tablespoons sugar, 1 teaspoon salt, and onions, and add to pan. Stir to coat all onions with butter mixture, and on low heat cook onions until caramelized (about 30 to 40 minutes), stirring occasionally. Once onions are caramelized, place in bowl, return pan to heat, and add bacon to pan. Cook bacon until crisp. Remove from pan and place on paper towels to remove excess fat. Crumble bacon and add to onions.

Prepare pasta according to package and set aside, reserving 2 cups of pasta water. In a large bowl, mix the pasta with onions, bacon, cranberries, dressing, and goat cheese. Chop cashews and add to pasta salad. Stir until combined; pour into your favorite serving dish and enjoy!

Venison Chili

Serves 6 to 8

This chili can be made ahead of time for when the hunting club spends the weekend together and everyone is famished and ready for a hearty meal at the end of a long day. Every hunter knows they must eat what they hunt, and there is always plenty of fresh venison to go around for this shared community meal.

4 tablespoons butter

1 red onion, chopped

4 cloves garlic, minced

4 tablespoons dark brown sugar

3 cups merlot

4 tablespoons red wine vinegar

4 tablespoons tomato paste

4 cups chicken stock

1 teaspoon ground cumin

½ teaspoon cayenne pepper

½ teaspoon chili powder

2 tablespoons chopped fresh cilantro

4 tablespoons extra virgin olive oil

10 slices cooked bacon, crispy, diced

2 pounds venison stew meat, trimmed, finely diced

2 cups canned black beans, liquid drained

Salt, to taste

Melt the butter in a large pot, stir in the onion and garlic, and sauté for 3 to 4 minutes. Stir in the brown sugar and sauté for 2 to 3 more minutes. Then stir in the red wine, vinegar, tomato paste, chicken stock, cumin, cayenne pepper, chili powder, cilantro, and salt. Simmer for 30 to 35 minutes, or until the mixture is reduced by about half.

Meanwhile, heat the oil in a large skillet over medium-high heat. Stir in the bacon and fry for 3 to 4 minutes, or until the bacon is browned. Move the bacon to one side of the skillet and add the venison to the empty side of the skillet. Season the meat with salt to taste and sauté the meat for 15 minutes, or until well browned. Stir in the beans and toss all together. Transfer this mixture to the simmering pot. Mix everything together thoroughly and let simmer for about 20 more minutes.

Brooklyn-Style Six-Foot Italian Hero

Anthony Musetti *(Marshall's Creek, Pennsylvania)*
Serves 36

I've been riding the same Harley since I was seventeen years old. Now I'm fifty-seven, and besides my wife and family, it remains one of my great loves. My other passion is cooking. For many years I catered the lunch for my Harley Davidson Riding Club's "Christmas in July" Toy Run. About fifty motorcycles, with their riders all bearing gifts for the children at the Kid's Peace Home, would escort Santa Claus. The kids would hear us coming and line up along the sides of the driveway. As we rode they'd cheer us on all the way to the parking lot, then come running out in awe to greet us. At that point Santa would climb down from his sled and hand out the presents we'd brought. It was such a great feeling to give to these children who had little else. Afterward everyone would get back on their bikes and get together with their own families to share a meal. We also organized raffle baskets and a fifty-fifty. All the proceeds from the sales would be donated to the Home, as well. You only need eight six-foot heroes to feed one hundred people.

6-foot Italian hero bread
8-ounce bottle Wish-Bone® Italian dressing
½ pound provolone cheese, sliced
½ pound salami, sliced
¼ pound mozzarella cheese, sliced
½ pound pepperoni, sliced

1½ pounds cappicola ham, sliced thin
3 sliced yellow onions
4 beefsteak tomatoes, sliced
3 cups lettuce, shredded
Salt, to taste
Pepper, to taste
Garlic salt, to taste
Oregano, to taste

Slice the Italian bread and place the bottom on a 6-foot piece of wood, precut for the purpose of bearing the weight of the sandwich. Pour ½ the bottle of the dressing along the entire surface of the bread. Place the cheeses, meats, onions, tomatoes, lettuce, and spices in the order listed above. Pour the remainder of the Italian dressing over the lettuce. Place the top of the bread on the hero. Slice and wrap in cellophane until ready to serve.

Variations
You may use Homemade Italian Dressing (see page 57), Italian Basil Pesto Sauce (see page 58), or balsamic vinegar and extra virgin olive oil in place of the bottled dressing.

Homemade Italian Dressing

1 cup red wine vinegar
1⅓ cups extra virgin olive oil
2 tablespoons water
½ tablespoon garlic powder
½ tablespoon onion powder
½ tablespoon sugar or stevia

1 tablespoon dried oregano
½ teaspoon freshly ground
   black pepper
½ teaspoon dried basil
½ tablespoon dried parsley
1 tablespoon sea salt

Pour the wet ingredients into a bottle or Mason jar. Then, using a funnel, add the dry ingredients. Cover and shake. Use and refrigerate any remainder for future use.

One teaspoon of dried herbs equals 1 tablespoon of fresh herbs. Measure ⅓ teaspoon of powdered spices for 1 tablespoon of fresh spices.

Italian Basil Pesto Sauce

¼ cup pine nuts
2 ounces fresh basil leaves
2 cloves garlic
8 tablespoons extra virgin olive
oil

⅓ cup romano cheese, grated
¼ cup parmesan cheese, grated
Sea salt and freshly ground
pepper, to taste

Using an ungreased skillet, toast the pine nuts until golden and then cool. Wash, dry, and chop the basil. Place the pine nuts, basil, garlic, and olive oil in a blender and puree until creamy. Stir in the cheeses; season with salt and pepper. You will need 8 ounces to use on an entire Italian hero.

Using the recipe above, add ½ cup sun-dried tomatoes, chopped. Reduce the amount of fresh basil to 2 tablespoons. Use one garlic clove instead of two. Process in a blender or food processor, and voila: you have sun-dried tomato pesto.

BBQ for Everybody

Anthony Musetti *(Marshall's Creek, Pennsylvania)*

Serves 200

> The Marshall's Creek Volunteer Fire Department throws a big barbecue every summer. It's a small town, so everybody comes. They make their own barbecue pit out of a 55-gallon metal drum that they cut in half lengthwise, after which they reattach one half to the other with hinges to make a flap, and weld bars across the top of one half to lay the grills on. The most difficult part of the cooking process is not the cooking itself; it's the making of the pit!

110-pounds strip steak, each cut into 12-ounce pieces

1 case barbecue sauce (or your own homemade)

Marinate the steaks overnight. Start your barbecue pit and grill.

Red Potato Salad with Bacon

Anthony Musetti *(Marshall's Creek, Pennsylvania)*

Serves 8

> When you are making this for a firehouse full of people you can increase the proportions of the ingredients considerably.

10 red potatoes
4 hard-boiled eggs
1 stalk celery, chopped fine
¾ cup scallions, greens on,
   chopped

6 slices cooked bacon
1 cup mayonnaise
2 tablespoons sour cream
Kosher salt and freshly ground
   pepper, to taste

Boil the potatoes in salted water for 15 minutes. Drain and partially cool. Mix in the ingredients in the order shown. Refrigerate overnight and serve.

Carrot Raisin Salad

Mary Carlin *(East Meadow, New York)*

Serves 8 to 10

> My mother-in-law made this salad whenever she had a barbecue. It is truly a guilty pleasure with the added sugar. This is perfect for a large group of neighbors at your block party, as it is easy, quick, and can be made a day ahead, leaving you plenty of time to meet and greet everyone.
> —*Monica*

4 cups shredded carrots
1½ cups raisins
¼ cup mayonnaise

2 tablespoons sugar (or equivalent stevia)
1 teaspoon apple cider vinegar

Toss carrots and raisins. Combine mayonnaise and sugar well; add vinegar and mix. Stir into carrot mixture.

Pony Camp Spirals

Kathleen Gallagher *(Oakdale, New York)*

Serves 12

As a young girl, my love for horses always found me at the stable, working long days for nothing but the opportunity to ride. Just working with and caring for these majestic animals brought such inner peace. Once a pony girl, always a pony girl!

When my daughter Tracy showed the same love for horses at a very young age, I knew that horses would always be a significant part of our lives. Horse shows, horse friends, pony parties, pony camp—everything we played, wore, read, or did had some connection to horses.

We were fortunate to have found a great home for our horse along with a great horse family at Willow Rock Farm. My dear friend Johnna, who is the owner/operator of the farm, got us all involved in the Old Suffolk Pony Club, a chapter of the United States Pony Club, at which many of our equestrian Olympians have passed through.

Summertime means Pony Camp to horse-loving kids. Johnna and I knew that we could build a great Pony Camp for the members of the club. We kicked it up a notch. The camp became a sleepover camp with breakfast, lunch, and dinner provided. I prepared and catered the meals. I always tried to keep the meals healthy, fun, and appealing to the eye as well as the palate. Not only did the most finicky eater gobble every bit of food down, but the parents and some friends usually found their way to the meal table as well. All raved that the best food one could eat could be found at Willow Rock Farm's Pony Camp.

For sun-dried tomato wrap:

1 package sun-dried tomato
  wraps
1 (12-ounce) package frozen
  spinach, drained, excess
  liquid squeezed out
1 cup sour cream
1 package dried vegetable soup
  mix

1 red bell pepper, roasted, cut in
  strips
1 small eggplant, roasted, cut in
  strips
1 avocado, sliced

Mix spinach, sour cream, and soup mix, then spread thin layer of the mixture over the entire wrap. Take 1 strip of pepper and lay it across the wrap. Roll once, then take avocado and eggplant and roll to the end of the wrap. Slice into 1-inch pieces; makes about 6 wraps.

For whole wheat wrap:

1 package whole wheat wraps
1 jar honey mustard spread
½ pound Monterey Jack cheese,
  sliced

½ pound Ovengold® turkey,
  sliced
2 cups fresh baby spinach,
  chopped

Spread mustard over entire wrap. Layer the cheese, turkey, and spinach three-fourths of the way across the wrap. Roll tightly right to the end. Cut into 1-inch pieces. Makes about 6 wraps.

For spinach wrap:

1 package spinach wraps
2 medium-size cans solid white
  meat tuna
4 tablespoons mayo

1 teaspoon apple cider vinegar
1 stalk celery, trimmed, finely
  chopped
2 cups baby spinach

Prepare tuna salad using tuna, mayo, vinegar and celery. To make the spiral, layer in spinach and 3 tablespoons tuna and wrap. Slice into 1-inch pieces. Makes about 6 wraps.

▪ You can substitute chicken or shrimp salad in this wrap.

Chicken Salad

1 large (12½-ounce) can chunk chicken breast

3 tablespoons mayo

2 cups shredded cole slaw mix

1 teaspoon apple balsamic vinegar

2 cups baby spinach

Mix salad ingredients. Add spinach and wrap as above.

Shrimp Salad

2 cups cooked baby shrimp, thawed

1½ teaspoons horseradish

4 tablespoons ketchup

2 tablespoons mayo

1 stalk celery, trimmed, finely chopped

2 cups baby spinach

Mix salad ingredients. Add spinach and wrap as above.

Warm Tuscan Pasta Salad

Roland Iadanza *(Commack, New York)*

Serves 6

1 pound fresh rigatoni
⅓ cup olive oil
1 clove garlic, minced
1 tablespoon balsamic vinegar
14 ounces artichoke hearts with stems
8 thin slices prosciutto, julienne
½ cup oven-roasted tomatoes, thinly sliced
¼ cup fresh basil leaves, chiffonade

2 cups baby arugula (rocket leaves)
¼ cup pine nuts
¼ cup Kalamata black olives (pitted)
Rosemary, sage, sea salt (from Italy), or sea salt mixed with fine chop of rosemary and sage

Blanch off rigatoni in salted water, al dente (firm). Drain thoroughly and transfer to serving bowl.

While pasta is cooking, whisk together oil, garlic, and balsamic vinegar. Toss dressing through hot pasta. Allow to cool slightly.

Add artichoke, prosciutto, oven-roasted tomatoes, basil arugula, pine nuts, and olives. Toss all ingredients until well combined. Season with sea salt, rosemary and sage to taste. Arrange in a bowl or platter, mounding up as high as possible for presentation.

Macaroni Salad

Harry Myers *(Lipan, Texas)*

Yields 2 quarts

4 cups uncooked elbow
   macaroni
1 cup mayonnaise
2 tablespoons white vinegar
2 tablespoons sugar
1 teaspoon salt

1 teaspoon black pepper
1 green pepper, chopped
1 carrot, shredded
1 medium onion, chopped
1 celery stalk, trimmed and
   chopped

Cook elbows for 8 minutes and set aside; they will be added later. Blend the other ingredients in a large bowl with a whisk until the mayonnaise curdles and the vinegar is smooth. Drain macaroni and mix into the bowl with the dressing. Place in containers and refrigerate overnight. The flavors will blend and absorb in the macaroni.

Part III:

APPETIZERS AND TAPAS

APPETIZERS AND TAPAS

Small-plate restaurants, providing diners with a number of small appetizers to share among themselves, have been popping up everywhere. Favoring little tastes of savory treats, the method is in line with our current nationwide trend of smaller portions. Allowing for many diverse dishes, as opposed to just one, the dining experience it provides takes you back to sharing food at Szechuan restaurants in the 1960s in Chinatown.

Call them tapas, call them hors d'oeuvres, these tasty preludes like Stuffed Mushrooms with Kale (pg. 75) can be passed around easily at a networking meeting, or served to a large group at a fundraiser, welcoming everyone to the beginning of an evening of fine dining. Tuna Tartar for Edible Asian Spoons (pg. 85), savory South Shore Crab Cakes (pg. 35)—so long as they are as delicious as they are easy to eat, it lets attendees quickly get back to their conversations.

The New York Press Association holds its annual awards ceremony celebrating weekly newspapers each spring, up in Saratoga Springs, home of legendary horse racing and the origin of the potato chip. Newspaper publishers, editors, marketing and sales professionals, photographers and journalists gather at the cocktail parties, luncheons, and dinners to praise each other's work and share workshops, trade tips, innovations in the field, and the challenges facing print media today. The staffs of these publications live within the communities they publish for, making the stories about fundraisers, soccer matches, boat races, and food festivals extremely compelling to their readers.

Of course, with all the hard work of reporting a story comes a very positive aspect: the reporters and photographers attend said fundraisers, bake sales, chili contests, and community fairs, and get to sample the food, often home-cooked, farm-raised haute cuisine of that community, like hot Cinco de Mayo Jalapeño Poppers (pg. 70) served at the many Mexican festivals held annually in May.

Cinco de Mayo Jalapeño Poppers

Yields 60

The North Shore-LIJ Hospital has locations throughout Long Island. Not only does it hold major fundraisers to add to the hospital's products and services, but it also gives back to its communities in a big way. Supporting street fairs, promoting good health through its health fairs, and sponsoring various events—the music, dancing, and food all reflect the chosen themes. This past year, one of its themes was Cinco de Mayo, which many embraced for the exuberance it elicits. This is just one of the appetizers found at such an event, cooked up by one of the community restaurants.

30 jalapeño peppers
2 (8-ounce) packages cream
  cheese, softened to room
  temperature
12 ounces shredded cheddar
  cheese
1 cup flour
¼ teaspoon salt

¼ teaspoon ground black pepper
⅛ teaspoon paprika
⅛ teaspoon chili powder
⅛ teaspoon garlic powder
1 cup milk
1 cup seasoned breadcrumbs
1 quart of oil, for frying

Slice jalapeños in half lengthwise. Use a spoon to scrape out the pith and the seeds inside of the peppers. In a bowl, combine cream cheese and cheddar cheese and stir until well blended. Use a spoon to fill each pepper half with the cream cheese blend.

Prepare seasoned flour by placing the flour into a small, shallow bowl. Add salt, pepper, paprika, chili powder, and garlic powder to the flour. Blend the spices into the flour until it has a uniform appearance. Place milk into a separate shallow bowl. Dip stuffed jalapeños into the seasoned flour, and then roll into the seasoned flour. Place floured peppers on a baking sheet with a rack. Let the peppers "dry" for about 10 minutes. This step is crucial for the peppers. The flour layer will help the stuffing to remain inside the pepper, and give the breadcrumbs something to hold on to.

Pour breadcrumbs into a separate bowl. Dip floured jalapeño peppers into the milk, and then into the breadcrumbs. Place peppers back on the rack. Preheat oil to 350°F degrees. Dip peppers into the milk and breadcrumbs for a second time. Go ahead and dip all; this should be enough drying time for the coating. The breadcrumb coating needs about 5 minutes to dry. Fry peppers, one or two at a time, until golden brown (1 to 2 minutes). Remove from oil and drain on a baking rack. Maintain oil to 350°F and cook until golden brown.

Roasted Salmon Stuffed with Spinach, Feta, and Ricotta

Serves 4

1 (2-pound) center-cut boneless, skinless salmon fillet
1 cup ricotta cheese
1 cup crumbled feta cheese
¼ cup mozzarella, shredded
½ teaspoon multicolored pepper, divided
1 tablespoon Dijon mustard
1 cup baby spinach, divided
¼ cup black olives, sliced thin
2 teaspoons extra virgin olive oil, plus extra for baking sheet
2 teaspoons fresh dill, chopped
2 teaspoons fresh oregano, chopped
Sea salt, ground fine, divided, to taste

Preheat oven to 450°F. Butterfly salmon, and then mix the cheeses until well blended. Sprinkle the salmon with some of the salt and pepper, and then spread the fillet with the Dijon. Arrange half of the spinach and half of the olives over the top, leaving at least an inch of border around the edges for easier rolling. Spread cheese mixture on top of the spinach and olives, and then do another layer of spinach and olives. Starting from one of the long sides, carefully roll salmon, pushing the stuffing back in if a little escapes. Gently tie with kitchen string.

Transfer salmon to your oiled baking sheet. Brush the top and sides with oil, salt, and pepper. Sprinkle the dill and oregano over the top and place in the oven for 20 to 30 minutes. Let the salmon rest a few minutes before removing string and serving.

Teriyaki Sesame Chicken Skewers

Serves 15

This dish was my son's favorite, all the way from middle school right up until today. The early days of bringing him to community events like the Brooklyn Botanic Garden's Cherry Blossom Festival exposed him to the diverse cuisines available in the melting pot that is our nation.

15 (8-inch) bamboo skewers

Marinade

8 ounces teriyaki sauce

3 tablespoons sesame oil

1 minced garlic clove

Juice of ½ lemon

1½ teaspoons confectioner's sugar

Chicken

1 pound chicken thighs, deboned, skin off

1 tablespoon sesame seeds, toasted

1 bunch scallions, sliced thin

Soak bamboo skewers in water for 1 hour to keep them from burning during cooking. Mix all marinade ingredients together in a container or in large resealable plastic bag. Cut chicken into ½-inch strips before placing them in the marinade. Cover and refrigerate for at least 1 hour.

Preheat oven to 375°F. Thread each chicken strip on a skewer close to the end of the tip, and line up on a baking pan. Bake for about 30 minutes, or until fully cooked through. Sprinkle with sesame seeds and scallions before serving.

Everybody's Fiesta Seven-Layer Dip

No fiesta would be complete without this rich, spicy dip. Everyone will go to this first at the buffet table. Adjust the heat by using less of the green chilies, especially if there will be kids at the gathering. Also, we suggest keeping a bottle of hot sauce on the table, just in case someone feels the need for extra heat. This would be perfect for your community center's Cinco de Mayo celebration, or to raise money for new sports equipment.

1 (10-ounce) can diced tomatoes
1 (10-ounce) can green chilies, diced, drained, liquid reserved
1 (16-ounce) can refried beans
1½ cups guacamole
1 (16-ounce) container sour cream
½ tablespoon chili powder
¼ tablespoon cumin
⅛ tablespoon seasoned salt
⅛ teaspoon oregano
⅛ teaspoon cilantro
1 cup cheddar and Monterey Jack, shredded
1 (2¼-ounce) can black olives, sliced, drained
¼ cup scallions, sliced thin
1 large bag tortilla chips
Bottle of hot sauce (optional)

Mix the tomatoes (reserve and set aside ½ cup of the tomatoes), green chilies, and the reserved liquid of the chilies with the beans. Spread bean mixture in an 8 x 8-inch glass baking dish. Top with guacamole. Mix together sour cream and chili powder, cumin, seasoned salt, oregano, and cilantro, and then spread over guacamole. Top evenly with layers of cheeses, olives, scallions, and reserved tomatoes. Chill. Serve with your favorite tortilla chips.

Stuffed Mushrooms with Kale

Serves 8

Thank goodness: healthy, green, leafy kale is now sold in pre-packaged and prewashed servings in most any grocery store! Before now, it was a laborious and daunting task to properly prepare kale, much less cook it for the long amount of time necessary to tenderize it. A task worth taking on, certainly: the monumental nutritional benefits outweighed the sheer amount of prep work. Thankfully, it is now easy to work with, and can be added to recipes as you would spinach.

24 small to medium-size white mushrooms
4 cups fresh kale
½ stick salted butter
½ yellow onion, chopped fine
3 cloves garlic, finely chopped
½ bunch fresh parsley, stems removed, chopped fine

½ cup parmesan cheese, grated
½ cup mozzarella cheese, shredded
¼ cup extra virgin olive oil
2 lemons
Salt and freshly ground black pepper, to taste

Wash mushrooms and remove stems. Dry whole mushrooms with paper towels and line up on cookie sheet. Chop stems well.

Using prewashed kale, trim away the stems, and then chop. Melt butter and add the mushroom stems, cooking for 1 minute. Mix in onion and cook for another minute, before adding the kale. Cook until just tender. Remove from heat and place in a mixing bowl. Add garlic, parsley, parmesan, mozzarella, and salt and pepper, mixing after adding each ingredient. Stuff each mushroom with equal amounts of mixture and bake in a 350°F oven for 30 to 40 minutes. Brush lightly with oil and place under a broiler for 1 to 2 minutes, keeping the oven door open so as not to burn. As soon as they come out, squeeze lemon juice over each one and serve warm.

Tempura Mushrooms

Serves 8

After a Little League game, all the parents on the team get together with everyone for a Japanese meal. Tempura-anything is always a kid-friendly dish and this one is no exception. Getting together after the games has brought everyone closer, and many of us remain friends to this day. Of course, as with all fried foods, this is a special-occasion dish; too much fried food slows down the team.

1 pound mushrooms

Marinade

5 tablespoons sherry

3 tablespoons soy sauce

2 tablespoons teriyaki sauce

2 teaspoons clover honey

2 teaspoons ginger, freshly grated

2 garlic cloves, crushed

½ bunch scallions, sliced extra thin

Batter

1 egg white

2 tablespoons flour

4 tablespoons sparkling water

½ cup sunflower oil (to fry)

Remove the stalks from mushrooms and chop fine. Mix the marinade ingredients with the stalks and pour over the mushroom caps. Marinate 4 hours.

To prepare the batter, beat the egg white and flour. While continuously beating, gradually add the water until the batter is slightly thickened. Heat 1 inch of oil in a deep frying pan. After draining the marinated mushrooms, dip them in the batter and deep fry, several at a time, for 2 to 3 minutes. Remove to paper towels with slotted spoon to drain off excess oil. Serve immediately with dipping sauce.

Pork Empanadas

Yields 40 pieces

Latin dancing, be it salsa, meringue, or cha cha, works up an appetite. The Long Island Dance Connection brings together dancers of all ages who move to the styles of the band Mambo Loco. You will regularly see generations mixing it up on the dance floor. Throughout the year, dancers get together at the newly renovated Riverhead Theater, a massive undertaking that took years of fundraising and renovations, to promote the North Shore of Long Island. It takes on a supper-club atmosphere, complete with a stage and dance floor up front and rows and rows of intimate tables for parties of two to twenty, all while featuring great food, music, and fun. Several towns endeavor to incorporate several events, such as the evenings of dance and cuisine at area restaurants, along with tours of local wineries. It's all about people working together to make it a success!

½ cup cream cheese
½ cup salted butter, softened
1½ cups flour
¾ pound ground pork
1 small yellow onion, finely
    chopped
1 chicken bouillon cube,
    dissolved in ¼ cup warm
    water

1 teaspoon ground allspice
¼ teaspoon ground nutmeg
⅛ teaspoon ground cloves
¾ cup mashed potatoes
2 large eggs, beaten

Beat cream cheese and butter until fully blended. Gradually add flour, mixing well. Once it has taken shape into a ball, refrigerate for at least 1 hour. Brown meat and onions. Stir in bouillon and spices. Remove from heat. Add potatoes; mix well. Cool completely.

Preheat oven to 400°F. Roll out chilled dough on a floured board to ¼-inch thickness. Cut dough into 40 rounds, each 3 inches.

Using 1½ teaspoons at a time, place meat mixture onto center of each dough round; brush edge with egg. Fold in half, pressing the edges together with a fork to seal. Place on a greased baking sheet. Prick small holes in tops to vent as you would for a pie and brush with the remaining beaten egg. Bake for about 20 minutes, or until golden brown.

Buffalo Chicken Bites

2 large chicken breasts, shredded
2 tablespoons buffalo chicken wing sauce
4 teaspoons bleu cheese dressing
3 ounces cream cheese, softened
1 tablespoon butter, softened
¾ cup cheddar cheese, shredded, divided
2 cans refrigerated pizza dough
¼ to ½ cup extra virgin olive oil (for greasing pan and brushing)
1 cup bleu cheese dressing
⅓ cup buffalo chicken wing sauce

Mix chicken, 2 tablespoons buffalo sauce, 4 teaspoons bleu cheese dressing, cream cheese, butter, and ½ cup cheddar cheese. Roll each can of pizza dough each into a 12 x 8-inch rectangle. Cut each rectangle of dough into 24 squares, for a total of 48 pieces. Place 1 teaspoon of chicken mixture onto each square. Lift up each square and wrap the dough around the toppings, squeezing the seams shut. Place seam-side down on a lightly greased cookie sheet. Brush with olive oil and top with remaining ¼ cup of cheddar cheese.

Bake 8 to 10 minutes in a preheated 450°F oven or until lightly golden brown. Serve warm with remaining bleu cheese dressing, buffalo chicken wing sauce for dipping, and celery sticks.

Spicy Shrimp

Serves 8

⅓ cup Italian dressing

1½ pound large uncooked shrimp, deveined and peeled

¼ cup orange marmalade

3 tablespoons freshly squeezed orange juice

½ teaspoon orange rind, grated

1 garlic clove, crushed, chopped fine

3 tablespoons chipotle peppers in adobo sauce, chopped

¼ cup cilantro, finely chopped

1 tablespoon red pepper flakes

Heat the dressing. Add shrimp and cook for 4 to 5 minutes. Stir to mix dressing and shrimp well.

Add the marmalade, orange juice, orange rind, garlic, and peppers; cook another 3 minutes or until shrimp are done. Garnish with cilantro and red pepper flakes.

Orange Marmalade

2¼ pounds oranges
2 small tangerines
2 lemons

12½ cups hot water
11½ cups sugar
⅓ cup orange liquor

Place a dampened cheesecloth in a bowl to capture juices. Cut oranges, tangerines, and lemons in half, and squeeze the juice from each into the bowl. Scrape out the the pulp and seeds from each juiced fruit and place in cheesecloth tied with kitchen string. Take the cheesecloth with seeds and pulp in it and squeeze out all juice, reserving it. Slice the peel crosswise and combine peel, pulp, and seed bag, reserved juice, and hot water. Bring to a boil over high heat.

Reduce heat and boil gently, stirring occasionally until peel is tender and mixture is reduced by nearly half (about 1½ hours). Remove from heat and transfer pulp bag to a sieve placed over a bowl. Extract as much juice as possible. Discard pulp bag and add that juice to cooked mixture. Measure out 10 cups, and then return to saucepan. If you are canning the marmalade, prepare your jars for canning using the standard canning process.

Bring the mixture to a boil over high heat, stirring constantly, and gradually stir in sugar, continuing to stir constantly until the mixture gels. This should take about 15 minutes. Once gel stage has been established, add liquor and continue to boil for 2 minutes. Skim off any foam. Ladle marmalade into receptacles. If canning marmalade, use your prepared jars and follow canning instructions.

You may also freeze the marmalade after using the portion needed for your recipe. Remember that, whether freezing or canning, always use sterilized receptacles and leave ¼ inch of space at the top to allow for expansion.

Asian Chicken Wings

Matthew Carlin *(Sayville, New York)*

Serves 4

2 tablespoons extra virgin olive
   oil
¼ cup chopped shallots
3 cloves garlic, minced
½ cup Blue Point lager beer
⅔ cup hoisin sauce

2 tablespoons soy sauce
1½ teaspoons hot red chili sauce
1½ pounds chicken wings
Mandarin oranges, for garnish
½ cup sesame seeds

Preheat oven to 425°F. Place the olive oil in a large pot over medium heat. Add the shallots and cook until softened (about 5 minutes). Add the garlic. Add the beer and hoisin, soy, and hot red chili sauces. Boil until thickened (6 to 8 minutes), stirring frequently.

Place the chicken wings in an even layer on a 9 x 13 baking dish. Pour the thickened sauce over them and bake for 15 minutes, turning the chicken over once. Continue to bake for about 15 to 20 minutes or until chicken is cooked through. Remove from oven to a serving platter that has been decorated around the edges with the mandarin oranges. Place the chicken wings in the center and sprinkle with sesame seeds.

Many people are serving boneless chicken wings, which are really white meat chicken strips that have been breaded like a chicken cutlet and fried, deep-fried, or baked. If using with the recipe above, follow all directions, but cook for an additional 20 to 30 minutes as the strips will take longer to cook than the bone in wings.

Simply Delicious Egg Rolls

Harry Myers *(Lipan, TX)*

Serves 20

> These egg-roll wrappers can be filled with a multitude of table foods or sandwich combinations, like macaroni and cheese, or ham and Swiss, making them the perfect finger-food plethora for party guests or as easy heated snacks. Their use is only limited by one's imagination and willingness to experiment. Can you think of some interesting fillings? This is a New York-style Cantonese egg roll, the most popular variety in most restaurants.

1 package egg-roll wrappers (about 20 to a package)
½ cabbage, shredded into strips ¼ x 2 inches, heavy, dark green outer leaves removed
1 carrot, shredded with potato peeler
1 celery stalk, thinly sliced across
¼ cup onion, cut into 2-inch strips ¼-inch wide

1 tablespoon ground ginger
1 tablespoon sugar
1 teaspoon salt
2 teaspoons garlic powder
3 tablespoons oyster sauce
1 tablespoon soy sauce
1 teaspoon onion powder
1 tablespoon cornstarch
2–3 tablespoons water
Oil for frying

Blend the ingredients thoroughly. If you wish to add small shrimp pieces, they will cook inside (make sure to check for doneness). Or, you may precook the shrimp before adding.

Heat oil to 365°F for deep-frying. Place heaping tablespoon of well-blended ingredients onto wrapper, as described in package instruction. Seal each one by brushing cornstarch and water around edges.

Before frying, fill and roll all the wrappers, and place aside to secure seals. Place three egg rolls in oil for 4 minutes each to cook inside. Remove with draining wide-screen scoop. Drain one at a time on paper towels. Dip in preferred sauce such as duck sauce or sweet and sour.

China Meets Italy

One day, Harry posted on Facebook that he'd been making all kinds of tasty finger foods using Chinese wonton skins with unconventional fillings. I immediately wanted to know how he'd done it. His answer?

"I use a deep fryer with a basket. The thermostat is the key to consistent batches, as opposed to pots with thermometers, which have to be carefully monitored with the stovetop adjustments."

As for the egg rolls, he went on to say, "I layer shredded mozzarella with cooked sausage, or meatballs and top it off with marinara. Brush the edges with water and fold like an envelope and roll and seal. Deep-fry for 2 minutes, turning until golden brown. The other is made with onion, green pepper, mushroom, and mozzarella (no marinara)."

Tuna Tartar for Edible Asian Spoons

Roland Iadanza *(Commack, New York)*

Serves 8

This simple, Asian-inspired tartar works wonderfully with the tanginess of the wasabi.

1 pound #1-grade tuna
2 teaspoons ginger, grated
5 teaspoons soy sauce
5 teaspoons orange juice

¼ teaspoon sesame oil
Wasabi edible spoons
1 packet micro greens

Dice tuna into small pieces (¼ inch). Grate ginger. Combine all other ingredients (except spoons and greens). Place 1 teaspoon of tartar on wasabi spoon and garnish with micro greens.

Shrimp and Banana Crostini

Chris Lang

Director of Culinary Services, Atria, Tanglewood *(Lynbrook, New York)*

A benefit at the Morgan Center for preschool children with cancer draws chefs from all over Long Island. This delectable recipe was made by student chefs who showed up that night, with their dishes "dressed to impress."

3 tablespoons ginger, chopped
3 tablespoons garlic, chopped, divided
Olive oil
1 teaspoon sesame oil
2 French baguettes, cut into 24 crostini rounds
4 tablespoons shallots, finely diced
6 ripe bananas
½ cup soy sauce, plus ½ cup water

2 to 3 tablespoons sriracha sauce
2 tablespoons honey
Juice of 2 limes
24 shrimp deveined, peeled, and tail off
1 bunch fresh cilantro, chopped
1 tablespoon lime juice
Micro greens
Finely diced red pepper and chives, for garnish
Salt and pepper, to taste

Crostini

Sauté ginger and 1 tablespoon garlic in olive oil with a teaspoon of toasted sesame oil until garlic and ginger are just browned. Let cool and brush the crostini round with infused oil mix. Toast crostini rounds in oven at 350°F until bread is lightly browned and set aside.

Bananas

Heat oil in a medium sauté pan and add shallots and 2 table-spoons garlic. Sauté for 3 minutes or until garlic is just browned. Add peeled bananas and cook for 5 minutes, or until bananas are soft and easy to mash. Add soy sauce, water, sriracha, honey, lime juice, and salt and pepper. Let liquid absorb and reduce. Set aside to cool.

Shrimp

Heat olive oil in a medium sauté pan. Add garlic and ginger. Add shrimp and sauté for 2 minutes. Turn shrimp and toss with fresh cilantro and 1 tablespoon lime juice. Cook shrimp until desired doneness and remove from heat.

To assemble:

Spread the banana mixture onto the crostini. Interlock two shrimp and place on top of the banana crostini. Top with some micro greens, diced red pepper, chives, and fresh cilantro. Bon appétit!

Morgan Center Benefit Signature Cocktail

Roland Iadanza *(Commack, New York)*

Makes 2 cocktails

Every benefit function should have a signature cocktail. The mint in this one, a favorite at the Morgan Center, makes it really refreshing, while the cranberry juice makes it bright and cheerful as it glistens in the candlelight.

2 ounces vodka
2 ounces cranberry juice
2 mint leaves

Juice of ⅓ lime
½ teaspoon agave nectar

Combine LiV vodka, cranberry juice, fresh lime juice, and agave nectar into shaker and mix well. Pour over ice, and garnish with a lime wedge and mint leaves.

Part IV:

ENTRÉES AND SIDES

ENTRÉES AND SIDES

There are so many interesting ways that people can get together to share a dinner. A picnic in the town park while listening to a Jimmy Buffet tribute band under a full moon; eating Teriyaki Sesame Chicken Skewers (pg. 73), or barbecued chicken and New Orleans-Style Dry-Rub Ribs (pg. 175) after a long day at the crafts fair, tasting your local restaurants' most-prized dishes at a fundraiser held in the ballroom at one of the local colleges—the list goes on. Common interests make for uncommonly good meals, and when it involves the whole community, personalities meld as much as do the flavors of the foods brought to the table, all of which add up to a more enjoyable event.

Take the Lenten soup supper: delicious soups and breads, being shared by Catholic churches everywhere. The mix of Polish or Italian, Hispanic or Asian members that make up the congregation makes for quite a selection of soups to choose from, like a Quick Chicken Vegetable Soup (pg. 38) or Hearty Mushroom Barley Soup (pg. 42).

The children are encouraged to make the soups with their parents, after which they serve the adults at the supper. Not only are parishioners invited, but often locals who may not have their own kitchen to prepare their own soup are happily included.

In many American towns, you'll find chapters of Kiwanians, Lions and Lionesses, Rotarians, Knights of Columbus, Key Clubs, Parent/Teacher Associations, Business Improvement Districts…people from all different walks of life that hold in common a desire to help others. Friends and neighbors, parents and teachers, students of all ages— all are part of the growing movement to lend a helping hand.

Each group carefully chooses which charities to focus on: the Lionesses give to the Guide Dog Foundation; Kiwanians offer scholarship money; the Chambers of Commerce hold tasting dinners with delicious dishes like Jamaican Jerk Chicken (pg. 113) to raise money for their events. Everyone learns to pay it forward, as one good deed leads to another and another.

Today's children have this awareness, as well. It can start as early as elementary school, as kids hold food drives to collect canned goods for a holiday meal, or serve a community Thanksgiving dinner with their parents at their local church, shelter, or food pantry to those less fortunate before going home to share their own family dinner. High school Key Clubs encourage their members to branch out and find projects within their communities, like decorating store windows during the holidays, or forming school choruses to volunteer to sing carols or serve hot chocolate and cookies over at the local nursing home or on a cold winter night during their town's annual Christmas tree lighting, spreading cheer to all their neighbors. Junior fire department volunteers follow their parents' lead, whether they are selling Christmas trees to raise money for new equipment, or learning life-saving techniques to help their neighbors. The next generation learns to nurture the desire to do good works from the one that has gone before.

Along with good works and good community spirit goes good food. Whether it is a spaghetti dinner of Fresh Rigatoni with Carbonara Sauce (pg. 122) or Caramelized Onion Pasta Salad (pg. 52) to raise money for a school trip or new choir robes, or a beef steak dinner held outdoors for a common cause, celebrating the triumphs of the community and working to make the world even better is an experience unlike any other.

People helping people, through good times and bad, brings added benefits, such as strengthening your family through strengthening your community, meeting friends with similar interests, and teaching your children the importance and the power of a simple act of kindness.

Pulled Pork Using a Dry Rub

Liz Finnegan *(Islip, New York)*

Serves 8

Civil War encampments are popular with history buffs, but make for a great community event as well. The days are spent often under the hot sun reenacting old battles, wearing traditional garb, and cooking over wood fires to entertain interested visitors from the surrounding comunity. At the end of the daily festivities, under much cooler conditions, the meal cooked over an open fire all day is shared with everyone in the camp. After the meal, the fires are doused, and the camps broken down. The twenty-first century regiment families retreat to their vehicles, parked nearby, leaving the eighteenth century behind for at least another weekend. Instead of using the oven to cook this dish, think of a cast-iron Dutch oven suspended over wood and simmering for hours until the day's mock battle has ended and the reenacters are rewarded with a succulent meal.

Dry Rub

3 tablespoons paprika

1 tablespoon garlic powder

1 tablespoon brown sugar

1 tablespoon dry mustard

3 tablespoons coarse sea salt

1 (6-pound) pork roast

Barbecue Sauce

1½ cups cider vinegar

1 cup yellow or brown mustard

½ cup ketchup

⅓ cup packed brown sugar

2 cloves garlic, smashed

1 teaspoon kosher salt

1 teaspoon cayenne

½ teaspoon freshly ground
    black pepper

Pan drippings from pork

12 biscuits

Dry Rub

Mix the paprika, garlic powder, brown sugar, dry mustard, and salt together in a small bowl. Rub the spice blend all over the pork. Cover and refrigerate overnight.

Barbecue Sauce

The next day, preheat oven to 300°F. Put the pork in a roasting pan and roast it for several hours (about 6 hours) or until the meat is falling apart. Combine the vinegar, mustard, ketchup, brown sugar, garlic, salt, cayenne, and black pepper and simmer (about 10 minutes). When the pork is done, take it out of the oven and remove to a large platter, which will enable you to then deglaze the pan using 1 cup of water, constantly scraping the bottom to release all the browned meat stuck on. Reduce to about half. Combine with the barbecue sauce and cook on the stovetop together (about 5 minutes). Using two forks, pull the meat into strands while it is still warm. Mix in about half of the sauce mixture with the pulled pork.

To serve, spoon the pulled pork mixture into each biscuit. Serve the extra sauce on the side or freeze and use for the next time.

Biscuits

Mrs. Carl Ownby *(Sevierville, Tennessee)*

> Biscuits are an important addition to any potluck or social event at which covered dishes are being served. Here are a few biscuit recipes that stem from the same initial biscuit mix, which you can pre-make and store, pulling out just when you need it.

7 to 8 cups self-rising flour   1½ cups shortening

Mix flour and shortening until crumbly like meal, and store in a covered container on a shelf (does not need refrigeration).

Freezer Biscuits
Combine 2 cups of mix and ½ cup of milk into stiff dough. Roll out on floured board, cut, and bake at 450°F for about 10 minutes. Remove from oven and freeze immediately. Bake as needed.

Soda Biscuits
Combine 2 cups of mix, ½ teaspoon of baking soda, and ½ cup of buttermilk. Mix well and bake at 450°F for approximately 15 to 20 minutes or until done.

Corn Bread
Combine 1 cup of mix, 1 cup of cornmeal, ½ teaspoon of baking soda, 2 eggs, and 1 to 1½ cups of buttermilk (this batter will be thin). Pour into a greased pan and bake at 425°F until done (30 to 40 minutes or until a toothpick comes out clean).

Stuffed Bleu Cheese Burgers

Serves 4

Our local cheese shop, American Cheese, has a large variety of locally made cheeses. Owner Erin Nicosia has had recipes in the Country Comfort series before, and I am so proud that she was able to take her farmer's market stand and turn it into a cheese shop offering meats, wines, jams, and all manner of cooking items, as well as an eat-in section. Her commitment to community has increased her popularity in Sayville, New York. She works together with wineries out on the North Fork of Long Island to pare her cheeses with their wines and with restaurants to showcase just what you can do with cheese as one of the main ingredients of your meal.

1½ pounds ground 80 percent-lean beef

2 teaspoons teriyaki sauce

½ red onion, diced fine

4 ounces bleu cheese, crumbled

½ pounds cooked bacon

Add the ground beef to the teriyaki sauce and onion and gently mix using your hands. Make eight equally sized ½-inch-thick patties. Make a slight indentation in the center of four of the burgers to hold the cheese. Divide the bleu cheese into four equal portions. Mold into circles, and set one in each of the four burger indentations. Top the cheese with the remaining burgers and seal the edges with your hands encasing the cheese. Refrigerate for about 4 hours.

When you are ready to grill the burgers, grill, covered, with vents open, until nicely marked and cooked to your liking. Remember not to press down, which could loosen cheese before time. Top with bacon and serve on whole wheat buns. Salt at the table as adding salt while grilling will cause too much shrinkage of the burgers.

Grilled Kentucky Bourbon Chicken

Liz Finnegan *(Islip, New York)*

Serves 12

Benefit dinners and community picnics aren't the only ways to get the community together for good food and good times. One thing that always draws a good crowd is war reenactments, a favorite of newcomers and history buffs alike. During a reenactment, soon after the morning meal is done, crowds begin to fill the park to witness the historical show. The soldiers, today representing the Third New York Regiment of the American Revolution, would initially be led by an "actor" portraying Major General Charles Lee (the father of Confederate Civil War general Robert E. Lee) and later on General George Washington.

Of course, there *are* some allowances for the the modern day, refrigeration among them. Without refrigeration on the mock battlefield, you would do the brining for this recipe at home beforehand; just follow the instructions for grilling over an open fire. The brining will help maintain the freshness of the chicken through the use of the bourbon and salt, just like those ingredients would preserve the fowl in olden times.

Brine

2 quarts water

½ cup bourbon, plus 1 tablespoon

¼ cup dark brown sugar, packed firm

3 tablespoons kosher salt

2 quarts ice water

1 tablespoon black peppercorns

1 tablespoon coriander seeds

3 bay leaves

3 garlic cloves, peeled

1 small onion, quartered

1 small Red Delicious apple, cored and quartered

1 lemon, quartered

1 (4-pound) whole chicken

Chicken

2 cups applewood chips

½ teaspoon freshly ground
mixed pepper

2 tablespoons extra virgin olive
oil (to brush on grill)

1 tablespoon butter, melted

½ cup chopped dried apricots
and unsalted shelled pistachio
nuts, skins removed to
garnish

Brine

Combine 2 quarts water, ½ cup bourbon, sugar, and kosher salt in a large Dutch oven, and bring to a boil, stirring until salt and sugar dissolve. Add ice water and next seven ingredients (through lemon), and cool to room temperature. Add chicken to brine; cover and refrigerate 18 hours, turning chicken occasionally.

Chicken

Before grilling, soak wood chips in water for 1 hour; drain. Remove the chicken from brine. Strain the brine and discard, reserving 2 apple quarters, 2 lemon quarters, 2 onion quarters, and garlic. Sprinkle inside of chicken with pepper and add reserved solids. Use a poultry truss to hold closed.

Use an indirect grilling method to grill the chicken. First, remove your grill rack, and set aside until ready to grill chicken. Heat one side to high and the other side with no heat. Pierce the bottom of an aluminum foil pan and place on the heated side. Heat element on heated side then add 1 cup wood chips to pan. Place a second aluminum foil pan, unpierced, on the unheated side of your grill. Pour 2 cups of water into that pan. Let chips stand for 20 minutes or until smoking; maintain a medium heat (about 250°F) on your gas grill.

Replace the grill rack and brush on a layer of extra virgin olive oil; this will cut down on sticking. Place whole chicken, breast-side up, on grill rack over foil pan on unheated side. Baste with remaining butter and bourbon. Close lid, and cook for 2 to 2 ½ hours. Halfway through cooking time, add the remaining wood chips. Let chicken rest for 10 minutes. Just before serving, sprinkle with dried apricots and pistachio nuts.

Fireman's Firehouse Chili

Serves 6 to 8

The firehouses along the south shore of Long Island joined in on the fun when they had their first ever Firehouse Chili Cook-off last summer. We all know that the firehouse is the place where these brave souls eat, sleep, and live as a family, able to be called upon in a moment's notice to fight a fire. The guys and gals take turns cooking for each other, and the result is some good eating amid a hidden treasure trove of foodies. Not only do they cook for each other, but our local Volunteer Department holds major fundraisers for people who need help. This chili is similar to what my husband enjoyed most: hot, hot, *hot!* You will find many versions of chili in this book, all reflecting the many ways one simple dish can be prepared, and the many ways neighbors help neighbors.

2 pounds ground beef
1 (15-ounce) can tomato sauce
1 cup water
1 teaspoon Tabasco® sauce
3 tablespoons chili powder
1 tablespoon oregano
2 onions, coarsely chopped
1 teaspoon cumin

1 teaspoon kosher salt
1 teaspoon cayenne pepper
1 teaspoon paprika
12 red peppers
4 to 5 chili pods
1 container sour cream
1 bunch scallions, chopped
Garlic, finely chopped, to taste

Sauté meat until browned. Combine all ingredients (except for sour cream and scallions) in a large sauce pot and simmer 2 hours. Top each serving with a dollop of sour cream and a tablespoon of scallions.

Duck L'Orange

Serves 8

During hunting season, whether for game like duck, goose, deer, or fish, hunting clubs get together, most often with a guide who is knowledgeable of the local terrain. The beauty of having such a guide is that once you've caught your duck, goose, salmon, or similar, they have the facilities to properly process your catch and store it frozen for you until you return home. If you don't intend to bring your catch home, they will often distribute it to local residents or restaurants. When eating the fish that your club have caught, some will even be prepared for you at your hotel restaurant, even as the rest is waiting for you to bring home.

2 (5½ to 6 pound) ducks, trimmed of excess fat; necks, gizzards, and hearts reserved
1 cup water
1 tablespoon vegetable oil
2 medium carrots, coarsely chopped
2 medium tomatoes, coarsely chopped
2 celery ribs, coarsely chopped
1 small leek, white and pale green parts only, coarsely chopped
1 small onion, coarsely chopped
2 cloves garlic, crushed, but not peeled

2 bay leaves
1 teaspoon dried thyme
3 tablespoons all-purpose flour
2 tablespoons tomato paste
1 quart chicken stock or low-sodium broth
1 cup dry white wine
5 navel oranges
⅓ cup sugar
⅓ cup cider vinegar
2 tablespoons currant jelly
2 tablespoons Grand Marnier®
2 tablespoons cold unsalted butter
Salt and freshly ground black pepper, to taste

Preheat the oven to 450°F. Cut off the first two wing joints of the ducks and reserve. Chop the necks into 2-inch lengths. Prick the ducks around the thighs, backs, and breasts. Season the ducks inside and out with salt and pepper. Set a rack in a very large roasting pan. Set the duck breasts up on the rack, as far apart as possible. Add the water to the pan and roast the ducks in the center of the oven for 20 minutes. Turn the oven temperature down to 350°F. Turn the ducks on their sides, propping them up by placing two large balls of foil between them, and roast for 30 minutes. Turn the ducks to their other side and roast for 30 minutes longer.

Meanwhile, in a large saucepan, heat the oil. Add the hearts, gizzards, wing joints, and necks and season with salt and pepper. Cook over moderately high heat, stirring, until richly browned, for 10 minutes. Add the carrots, tomatoes, celery, leek, onion, garlic, bay leaves, and thyme and cook, stirring, until softened, which should take about 5 minutes. Stir in the flour and tomato paste, and then gradually stir in the stock and wine. Bring to a boil, stirring, then reduce the heat to moderately low and simmer for 1 hour. Strain the sauce into a bowl, pressing on the solids.

Meanwhile, remove the zest in strips from one of the oranges. Cut the zest into a very fine julienne. In a small saucepan of boiling water, blanch the julienne for 1 minute. Drain and rinse under cold water; pat dry.

Halve and squeeze two of the oranges; you will need 1 cup of juice. Peel the remaining oranges (including the one you stripped the zest from) with a knife, removing all of the bitter, white pith. Cut in between the membranes to release the sections into a bowl.

In a medium saucepan, boil the sugar and vinegar over moderately high heat until the syrup is a pale caramel color (4 minutes). Gradually add the 1 cup of orange juice, then the currant jelly, and bring to a boil. Add the strained duck sauce and simmer over moderate heat to reduce slightly (8 minutes). Season with salt and pepper. Add the Grand Marnier and remove from the heat. Swirl in the butter, 1 tablespoon at a time.

Pour off the fat in the roasting pan. Turn the ducks, breast-sides up, and roast for 40 minutes longer. Remove the ducks from the oven and preheat the broiler. Broil the ducks 6 inches from the heat, rotating the pan a few times, until richly browned (about 3 minutes).

Insert a wooden spoon into the cavities and tilt the ducks, letting the juices run into the pan. Transfer the ducks to a platter and keep warm. Scrape the pan juices into a fat separator and pour the juices back into the roasting pan. Simmer over moderate heat, scraping up any browned bits and coagulated juices. Strain the contents of the roasting pan into the orange sauce.

Garnish the duck platter with the reserved orange sections and scatter the blanched zest over the ducks. Carve the ducks at the table and pass the sauce separately.

Grilled Chicken Thighs with Purple Plum/Mandarin Orange Salsa

Serves 8

1 dozen chicken thighs

4 teaspoons extra virgin olive oil, for grill

Sauce

2 cups ripe purple plums, chopped, skin on, divided

1 cup canned mandarin orange, juice drained

1 large jalapeno pepper, seeded and diced

4 tablespoons fresh basil, chopped

4 tablespoons red onion, chopped

¾ teaspoon kosher salt, divided

1 teaspoon plum balsamic vinegar

1 cup apple cider

2 teaspoons fresh lime juice

Dry Rub

4 tablespoons dark brown sugar

1 teaspoon roasted ground cumin

Stir together 1 cup plums, ½ cup orange, pepper, basil, onion, ¼ teaspoon salt, balsamic vinegar, and apple cider and cook in a saucepan until all liquid is absorbed, stirring often. Mix brown sugar, cumin, and remaining ½ teaspoon salt. Rub into the chicken.

Cook chicken on low on a prepared covered grill, turning often until done. Mix remaining 1 cup uncooked plums with ½ cup uncooked mandarin orange with the cooked plum/orange mixture; spoon over chicken and serve.

Grilled Salmon with Avocado/Mango Salsa

Serves 4

Seth, from The Fish Store in Bayport, New York, has sat on the Bayport Chamber of Commerce board of directors for years. Even after he and his wife were graced with twins, he never skipped a beat in organizing community events and fund-raisers. From open forums to carnivals, to price fixed lunch menus served during Chamber meetings, he is often the point person. Proceeds go to many different events the Chamber does throughout the year.

2 pounds fresh salmon

Heated Portion

1 tablespoon extra virgin olive oil

1 ripe mango, peeled, pitted, and diced

¼ cup water

1 teaspoon freshly squeezed lemon juice

Chilled Portion

1 tablespoon cilantro leaves, finely chopped

2 teaspoons mint leaves, finely chopped

1 tablespoon red onion, chopped fine

1½ tablespoons freshly squeezed lime juice

3 tablespoons extra virgin olive oil

1 large mango, peeled, pitted, and diced

1 large mango, peeled, pitted, and diced

1 avacado, pitted and diced

Kosher salt and multicolored freshly ground pepper, to taste

Heated Portion

Heat the olive oil, and add the mango. Cook for about 3 minutes until the fruit is very tender. Add water, bring to a boil, and remove from heat. Stir in lemon juice. Alternatively, if you are pressed for time, put all of the sauce ingredients into a blender and puree.

Chilled Portion

Mix 2 teaspoons of the cilantro, 1 teaspoon of the mint, the red onion, 1 tablespoon of lime juice, 2 tablespoons of olive oil, and salt and pepper. Set aside. In a separate bowl, add the mango, avocado, 1 tablespoon of olive oil, ½ tablespoon of lime juice, and the remaining cilantro and mint leaves, Mix gently. Combine all with heated portion and set aside. Grill the salmon. Spoon avocado/ mango mixture over each serving. Sprinkle with cilantro.

Shrimp with Snow Peas and Water Chestnuts

Serves 2 to 4

The family-owned JJ Dynasty Chinese restaurant in Oakdale, New York, is just one of the twenty-five or so restaurants that donate food to the Oakdale Chamber of Commerce's annual Taste of Oakdale, held in the historic ballroom and hunt room of Dowling College. It is one of the biggest and best events of the year, with Oakdale community members being involved in one way or another. The restaurants and delis supply trays of food; the flower shop supplies centerpieces; the local theater company, CM Performing Arts, sings show tunes; and the Dowling Jazz Ensemble plays terrific professional background swing tunes. Residents who aren't attending are there to help out and serve the several hundred people who do attend. The proceeds always go to Oakdale causes; a big chunk of money was donated as seed money to the newly formed Oakdale Historical Society. Thanks to the cooperation of all of the Oakdale businesses and institutions, this event is always a fun way to meet and greet your neighbors in a relaxed setting.

1 pound shrimp (uncooked)
¼ cup dry sherry
2 tablespoons soy sauce
2 tablespoons vegetable oil
1 tablespoon fresh ginger, peeled and minced
1 cup fresh mushrooms, sliced
½ pound snow peas, rinsed, stems and strings removed
½ cup sliced scallion
½ cup sliced water chestnuts
1 teaspoon cornstarch, dissolved in 3 tablespoons water
Hot cooked brown rice

Peel and devein shrimp. Combine the sherry and soy sauce and add shrimp. Marinate in the refrigerator for 30 minutes. Heat a pan and add the oil. This is similar to a Chinese stir-fry, so if you have a wok, now is the time to use it. Add ginger and stir-fry for 1 minute. Add the shrimp (reserving the marinade) and cook until light pink (2 to 3 minutes). Add mushrooms and snow peas and cook for 1 to 2 minutes, until the snow peas are bright green and crisp-tender. Add scallions and water chestnuts and stir-fry until just heated through. Add the reserved marinade and cornstarch mixture. Bring to a boil and cook until the sauce thickens. Serve with brown rice.

Beef Stew in a Bread Bowl

Mary Carlin *(East Meadow, New York)*

Serves 4

> This recipe is great for those who love a warm meal at the end of the day. The recipe can be increased as many times as needed to accomodate the whole Girl Scout troop, who have been out selling cookies and need to warm up after a long day.
> *—Monica*

3 pounds beef tips
1 yellow onion sliced
¼ cup teryaki sauce
2 cups beef stock
1 cup water

2 cups potatoes, diced
1 cup carrots, diced
1 tablespoon tomato paste
2 tablespoons rosemary
4 large pumpernickel rolls

Brown the beef tips with onion. Add teryaki sauce and cook 1 minute. Add beef stock, water, potatoes, carrots, tomato paste, and rosemary. Cook over medium heat about 1½ hours or until beef is fork-tender. Using a sharp knife, cut in a circular motion around the top of the rolls or small loaves of bread, removing the top. Pull bread out to form a bowl for the stew and place the pulled bread pieces to the side. Spoon the hot stew into the bread bowls and use the top and pulled bread pieces to dip into the stew.

Spinach and Chicken Stuffed Shell Casserole

Elizabeth Meyers *(Port Jefferson Station, New York)*

Serves 6 to 8

> Though my mom didn't have the time to volunteer, being a single, working mom with three children, she did regularly cook for our family gathering, which could get to be upward of sixty people. Known for her Italian specialties, she could replicate any recipe she followed and have it turn out just perfectly. This is a great dish for a family reunion.
> —*Monica*

18 large macaroni shells, for stuffing
¼ cup flour
½ cup milk
¼ cups chicken stock
1½ tablespoons tomato paste
2 teaspoons butter
½ white meat chicken, cooked, diced fine
2 cloves garlic, pressed
1 pound baby spinach, packaged, prewashed, chopped

2 cups ricotta cheese
3 tablespoons parmesan cheese, grated
2 eggs
3 tablespoons fresh parsley, chopped fine, divided
12 teaspoons chives, chopped
1 pinch nutmeg
¹⁄₁₆ teaspoon white pepper
½ cup mozzarella cheese, shredded

Preheat oven to 350°F. Prepare shells according to package directions for al dente consistency, drain, and set aside. Whisk the flour and milk together, then add in the chicken stock and tomato paste, and whisk. Bring to a boil, whisking constantly, then reduce heat and simmer for about 2 minutes to make a thickened sauce; set aside.

Melt butter in a large pan and add the chicken. Stir for a minute, stirring in the garlic, and then the spinach, cooking until the spinach is wilted. Remove from heat, and in a large bowl, mix with the cheeses (except mozzarella), eggs, parsley, chives, nutmeg, and pepper to create the filling. Stuff each shell with a teaspoon of filling, careful not to overstuff. Using half your sauce, cover the bottom of a baking dish, then place each shell seam-side down. Cover and bake for 30 minutes or until the sauce is bubbling up. Add the remaining sauce. Sprinkle on the mozzarella and bake uncovered an additional minute or until cheese is just melted. Sprinkle with parsley before serving (2 to 3 tablespoons to each person). Any leftover filling can be refrigerated and used to toss loosely with pasta for a nice homemade lunch.

Eleven-year-old Ashley Tuthill of Bellport, New York, was driving home with her parents when she saw a line of people waiting to enter a local church. Not understanding why anyone would line up to enter a church, she asked her parents about it, and was told that they were a group of less fortunate individuals and families coming to receive care packages.

Very taken aback by that realization, Ashley decided to start collecting food to donate to the church outreach center, saying to her parents, "We have so much; we should help in some way." She went about setting up collection spots at her parents' jobs, her school, and anywhere else she could think of. Ashley then put up fliers asking for donations of nonperishable food items with an explanation of why she needed them. In no time the collections grew, netting pasta; rice; beans; canned meats, vegetables, and fish; and jarred sauces, soups, stews, and fruits, with many of the items just perfect for several variations of comforting and tasty casseroles. Within weeks boxes of food were collected and ready to be delivered. It wasn't Christmas or any other holiday when one gives to another; it was just another day in the life of one little girl with a big heart who was compelled to help, had an idea, and acted upon it.
—*Monica*

Risotto Primavera

Donna Cermak *(Sayville, New York)*

Serves 4

> Donna was one of the many individuals who donated her time and recipes to the fund to build the newly expanded library in her community. This casserole can be made using many of the donations that were given to young Ashley's cause described above. Dried onion, jarred red peppers, canned mushrooms, grated cheese, and cooking wine all come in nonperishable alternatives, which were found in the care packages. There are also many community gardens that offer free vegetables to those in need during harvest season, so the zucchini and onions are also very accessible food items when you are stretching your dollar.
> —*Monica*

2 tablespoons extra virgin olive oil

1 medium yellow onion, thinly sliced

2 small zucchini, julienne sliced

1 red bell pepper, seeded and cut into thin strips

8 mushrooms, dried and thinly sliced

1 cup uncooked risotto rice

½ cup dry white wine

5½ cups chicken broth

4 tablespoons freshly grated parmesan cheese

Salt and pepper, to taste

In a large pan, heat the olive oil over medium heat until hot. Add the onion, and sauté for about 4 to 5 minutes, stirring often so as not to burn. Add the zucchini and bell pepper. Cook and stir 5 to 7 minutes, or until zucchini is tender and still crisp. Meanwhile, sauté the mushrooms in oil in a separate pan at medium-high heat and add to the vegetables when done. Remove the vegetables and set aside. Add rice and wine to the pan in which the vegetables were cooked, stirring until the wine is absorbed. Add 1 cup chicken broth. Cook, uncovered, stirring frequently, until absorbed.

(You may need to adjust the heat, depending on whether the rice is boiling too little or too much.) Add an additional cup of chicken broth. Cook, uncovered, stirring frequently until absorbed. Add the remaining ¾ cup stock, and cook until absorbed, stirring frequently. (Total cook time should be about 25 minutes, or until the rice is tender and mixture is creamy.) Stir in vegetables and parmesan cheese. Season to taste with salt and pepper.

You may also add sautéed shrimp to the risotto when ready to serve.

Jamaican Jerk Chicken

Serves 6 to 8

All throughout my son's childhood, we spent every day in our "backyard" of Brooklyn's Park Slope: Prospect Park, the Brooklyn Botanic Garden, the Brooklyn Museum, and the Prospect Park Zoo with the renovated carousel that hundreds of Brooklynites raised money for. There were always interesting community events, like Back to Brooklyn, when we met celebrities like Danny Kaye, former members of the Brooklyn Dodgers—we even got an autograph from Marisa Tomei!

Back to Brooklyn is an enormous community event, held on Grand Army Plaza each June, with vendor booths, balloons, and interesting people all promoting Brooklyn in one way or another. Nonprofits, restaurants, merchants, music, and even all the politicians come out. The event really has made a difference and helped Brooklyn become what it is today: thriving and bustling once again. For us foodies, we get to sample all kinds of cuisine, but the Jamaican specialties hold a place dear to my heart and palate.

For the brine:

2 gallons water (for brine)
6 whole cloves
¼ teaspoon allspice
½ inch ginger, peeled

1 cinnamon stick
¼ teaspoon nutmeg
1 teaspoon kosher salt
2 (4-pound) chickens

For the chicken:

½ cup fresh lime juice
3 tablespoons dark rum
2 tablespoons water
½ cup malt vinegar
10 scallions, chopped
5 cloves garlic, chopped fine
3 tablespoons dried thyme

2 habanera chilies, chopped
2 tablespoons extra virgin olive oil
5 teaspoons ground allspice
5 teaspoons ground ginger
5 teaspoons ground cinnamon
3 teaspoons ground nutmeg

2 teaspoons kosher salt

2 teaspoons ground black pepper

3 teaspoons dark brown sugar

1 cup ketchup

4 tablespoons soy sauce

Brine

Mix all ingredients together for brine. Skin the chickens and place them in brine overnight in the refrigerator. If you don't have a 2-gallon receptacle, divide brine recipe and place each chicken in 1 gallon of brine. In the morning, remove from brine; pat dry.

Chicken

Cut brined chickens in half lengthwise. Place in a roasting pan. Pour on the lime juice, turning to coat both sides. Set aside. Boil rum and 2 tablespoons water for 3 to 4 minutes, then place in a blender. To the blender, add vinegar and the scallions through the dark brown sugar and continue to blend. Using 2 tablespoons of your jerk seasoning, mix with the ketchup and soy sauce. Pour over chicken, spreading all over top and bottom. Cover and marinate in the refrigerator for 4 hours, turning occasionally. When ready to bake, preheat oven to 350°F. Remove chicken from marinade. Roast chicken, covered, 50 minutes, then remove cover and cook for an additional 5 to 10 minutes. Cut into pieces and serve.

Mock Jamaican Patties

Serves 12 to 24

For the meat filling:

1 small white onion, finely chopped

¼ teaspoon chopped Scotch bonnet pepper

2 tablespoons butter

½ pound lean ground beef

½ teaspoon curry powder

½ teaspoon dried thyme, crushed

½ teaspoon ground allspice berries

½ teaspoon salt

½ teaspoon freshly ground black pepper

¼ cup breadcrumbs

¼ cup beef stock

For the patties:

2 tubes Pillsbury Grands!® muffins

1 tablespoon curry powder

¼ cup water

1 egg, beaten

Meat Filling

Sauté onion and peppers in butter until softened. Add the beef, curry powder, thyme, allspice, salt, and pepper. Sauté until beef is browned. Stir in breadcrumbs and beef stock. Cover and simmer for 10 minutes, stirring once or twice until all the liquid is absorbed. Cool for about 10 minutes.

Patties

Lay muffin rounds out on a flowered surface. Flatten each one with a rolling pin or press flat with your hand. Place 1 tablespoon of the meat filling in the center of each pastry round. Moisten the edges of the circles with water, fold in half, and seal edges with the prongs of a fork and sprinkle with curry powder. Mix remaining water with the egg and brush the tops. Place on a greased cookie sheet or pizza stone. Bake in a preheated 350°F oven for 30 to 40 minutes or until golden brown.

Puerto Rican Pork Roast

Serves 6 to 8

My niece Stephanie, a mother of one precocious young boy, with another child on the way, discovered once she had become a mom that she was also a pretty good cook. Following in the Musetti tradition of knowledgeable foodies, she puts her best recipes up online for her whole extended family and friends to share, and is not afraid to ask questions about how to best prepare something she has never tried before. Her husband Chris, of Puerto Rican descent, loves her cooking and has said that one of the things that she *had* to learn to make was a proper pork roast. My mother-in-law Mary always used to say, "Cook the foods your husband grew up with and he will always come home."

8 cloves garlic, peeled
¼ cup salt
¼ cup black pepper
2 teaspoons chopped fresh
  oregano

3 tablespoons extra virgin olive
  oil
1 (10-pound) pork picnic roast
¼ teaspoon sazon
¼ teaspoon adobo

Preheat the oven to 425°F. Blend the garlic, salt, pepper, oregano, and olive oil until smooth. Pierce the pork with several ½-inch lengths. Insert the garlic paste into each one. Sprinkle with sazon and adobo. Place in a covered roasting pan. Bake for 1½ to 2 hours until no longer pink inside.

Fried Plantains

Serves 8

1 quart extra virgin olive oil,   2 plantains
    for frying

Preheat oil in a large, deep skillet over medium-high heat. Peel the plantains and cut them in half. Slice the halves lengthwise into thin pieces. Fry the pieces until browned and tender. Drain excess oil on paper towels.

Maple-Glazed Stuffed Roast Pork

Serves 2 to 4

2 tablespoons butter
1 apple, chopped
¼ cup raisins
1½ cups hot water
1 package (6 ounces) herbed
　Stove Top stuffing
1 pork loin (2 pounds),
　butterflied

2 tablespoons maple syrup
2 tablespoons Grey Poupon®
　mustard
1 teaspoon chopped fresh
　rosemary

Preheat oven to 350°F. Melt butter, add apples and raisins, and cook 3 minutes. Add water and stuffing mix; cover. Let stand for 5 minutes; mix lightly. Press mixture onto cut side of meat, leaving room at the edge to roll up jelly-roll style. Placing seam-side down, roast in greased pan. Bake uncovered for 1 hour. Mix syrup, mustard, and rosemary; spread over meat.

Bake an additional 30 minutes or until meat is done (internal temperature of 160°F). Let meat rest before slicing. Serve with biscuits.

Western Sky Rodeo BBQ Ribs

Serves 8 to 10

Cheyenne, Wyoming, is the home of Frontier Days, the Wild West festival I attended when I lived there as a child in the third grade. Back then, it was exciting, and kicked off with a parade, complete with horseback riding and a rodeo. That was over fifty years ago; the fairgrounds now include soccer matches, and there are a series of foot races. The food is the same though: tender ribs cooked to perfection, rubbed with spices and slow cooked. The whole community has to come together for a treat like that!

1 cup seasoned salt
1 cup garlic powder
1 cup black pepper
1 large rack pork spare ribs,
   about 6 pounds

1 to 2 bottles barbecue sauce,
   heated (recommended: Jack
   Daniel's® Barebecue Sauce)

Prepare grill. Mix seasoned salt, garlic powder, and black pepper together. Rub onto ribs (store excess rub in an airtight container). Place rack of ribs, rib-side down, onto grill. Cook for 15 minutes. Turn ribs over and cook for another 15 minutes. Remove ribs from the grill just before they are cooked to your liking. Empty barbecue sauce into a roasting pan. Transfer ribs to pan with heated sauce, cover, and let the ribs continue to cook for another 10 to 15 minutes. Serve with extra sauce on the side. Try with carrot or raisin slaw!

Chicken Chili with Garbanzo Beans

Serves 6 to 8

1 (4-pound) chicken, cut into 8 pieces
¾ cup chopped onion
2 tablespoons extra virgin olive oil
1 teaspoon kosher salt
1 tablespoon oregano
3 tablespoons chili powder
2 tablespoons cumin
1 large (15-ounce) can tomatoes, crushed
1 large (15-ounce) can tomato puree

1 tablespoon tomato paste
16 ounces water
2 (8-ounce) cans garbanzo beans, drained
1 (8-ounce) can white beans, drained
1 cup cheddar cheese, grated
½ cup fresh cilantro, chopped fine
1 tablespoon pickled jalapeño peppers, chopped (optional)

In a large sauce pot, sauté chicken and onion in the olive oil. Stir in salt, and sauté for 1 minute. Stir in oregano and sauté for 1 minute. Stir in chili powder and cumin, continuing to cook for 1 minute after each. Add the crushed tomatoes, tomato puree, tomato paste, and water. Stir.

Stir in the beans. Cover and cook 2 hours, stirring occasionally, adding more water if it gets too thick. When done, remove chicken pieces carefully from the chili pot and debone. Replace chicken pieces in the chili pot. Serve in a festive bowl topped with cheese, cilantro, and jalapeño peppers (optional).

White Bean and Turkey Chili

Serves 6

1 tablespoon extra virgin olive oil

2 cups diced yellow onion

1½ tablespoons chili powder

1 tablespoon garlic, minced

1½ teaspoons ground cumin

1 carrot, diced

1 cup roasted corn kernels

1 teaspoon dried oregano

3 (15.8-ounce) cans white beans, rinsed and drained

4 cups chicken stock

3 cups chopped cooked turkey

½ cup diced seeded plum tomato

⅓ cup chopped fresh cilantro

2 tablespoons fresh lime juice

½ teaspoon salt

½ teaspoon freshly ground black pepper

Heat oil in a large sauce pot. Add onion; sauté until tender. Add chili powder, garlic, and cumin; sauté for 2 minutes. Add carrot and corn. Add oregano and beans. Stir, then add broth. Simmer for 1 hour. Add turkey, and cook another 30 minutes. Remove from heat. Add diced tomato, chopped cilantro, lime juice, salt, and pepper.

Fresh Rigatoni with Carbonara Sauce

Roland Iadanza *(Commack, New York)*

Serves 4

The Morgan Center Event at Southward Ho Country Club in West Bay Shore, New York, is an annual benefit featuring top chefs, brewers, bakers, and wine makers—all for a great cause. It all started in 2003, when my niece Laura Kehl came to me with a request. She was teaching swimming to a five-year-old girl named Morgan, who was diagnosed with acute lymphoblastic leukemia at the age of two. Due to her suppressed immune system, Morgan could not interact with other children or go to preschool. She was truly affected by the lack of opportunity to learn and socialize. When she started kindergarten, Morgan's parents, Nancy and Rod Zuch, created The Morgan Center for preschool-age children battling cancer. This is just one of the many dishes created especially for this event—plentiful and delicious.

1 pound bacon, diced into
  ½-inch pieces
1 large Spanish onion, diced
  large
6 cloves garlic, sliced thin
1 quart heavy cream
6 leaves of fresh basil, in thin
  strips

2 pounds fresh pasta, rigatoni,
  fusilli, and/or radiatore
Sage, rosemary, and salt,
  to taste
Fresh ground black pepper,
  to taste
Freshly grated parmesan
  cheese, to taste

Cook bacon on medium heat in heavy-gauge sauce pot without adding any additional fat, and cook until bacon has started to brown. Add onions and cook until softened; add garlic and cook until slightly brown and "caramelized" (cooking the onions and garlic until the sugar comes out and caramelizes, adding a fuller, more complex taste). Add heavy cream and season with salt, rosemary and sage. Let it "reduce" (boil down) to a slightly thick consistency. The convection movements should have a glazed look and the cream should coat the back of a spoon when it is ready.

Turn off heat and add basil; stir in. Toss with fresh pasta and grated cheese. Add fresh ground pepper to taste. Enjoy! The reaction you will get from people when you make this dish will be amazing! Of course, when cooking for the benefit, this recipe was increased considerably.

Tricolor Fresh Tagliatelle with Gulf Shrimp

Chef Roland Iadanza *(Commack, New York)*

Serves 4

The Southward Ho Country Club was the best place to have The Morgan Center fundraiser, since both my niece and Morgan's family grew up there as members. Plus, many of the other members were eager to support this grassroots organization. Being a chef and associated with the American Culinary Federation, and in sales for Pasta People, I'd become friendly with Chef Alain De Coster, dining-room manager at the time, and Southward Ho Executive Chef Mike Lika. Together, we formed the Great Chef's Fundraiser to benefit The Morgan Center. Using my thirty-four years in the business provided me with many chef contacts who were eager to help.

Our major challenge was that the event was to be held on a Friday evening, which is a busy night in the food-service industry. We were thrilled that, after learning about The Morgan Center, many chefs made themselves available to attend. That first year, we had around ninety guests. This is one of the many dishes served. The fresh pasta coupled with the tender shrimp is a real crowd pleaser and goes a long way for a big event.

2 large zucchini
2 large carrots
12 Gulf shrimp U15
Wondra® flour
16 ounces fresh pasta sheets, for tagliatelle pasta (plus flour for dusting)
4 tablespoons extra virgin olive oil

Basil butter
4 roasted garlic cloves, plus extra for garnish
1 cup grated pecorino-romano cheese
Basil leaves, for garnish
Salt and fresh ground black pepper, to taste

With a vegetable peeler, cut zucchini and carrots in long, thin ribbons. Bring a large pot of water to a boil and add salt. Season and dust shrimp in flour; sauté shrimp until pink and slightly firm. Set aside. Roll up or fold pasta sheets and cut fresh tagliatelle a little thinner than fettuccine. Cook in boiling salted water for 3 minutes, add zucchini and carrot ribbons, and let boil for 30 seconds. Reserve 1 cup of pasta cooking water. Drain well and add back to pasta pot.

Add olive oil, basil butter, roasted garlic, and shrimp to pot and toss over medium-high heat until pasta and vegetables are coated well. Swirl pasta and vegetables with a large fork or tongs in a circular motion and place on center of four plates. Place shrimp at three points around pasta. Grate pecorino-romano cheese over pasta and garnish with roasted garlic cloves and basil chiffonade. Preparing it for a crowd, increase ingredients.

Pan-Roasted Pork Tenderloin and Julienne Potato Cake with Havarti Cheese

Chef Roland Iadanza *(Commack, New York)*

Serves 6 to 8

Now in its eleventh year, The Great Chefs Event draws between 400 to 500 people and helps raise almost half the yearly operating expenses for The Morgan Center. Participants range from restaurants to country clubs, gourmet stores, assisted-living facilities, breweries, and pastry chefs, to name a few. Many food vendors also donate products. The dedicated people on our steering committee and advisory board participate to make this a great evening of food and drink for a very worthy cause. Ultimately our efforts give these young children with cancer the opportunity to socialize, learn, and have fun together.

2 pork tenderloins
Oil, for searing

Salt and fresh ground pepper, to taste

For the sauce:

Trimmings from pork tenderloin
Oil, for cooking
Mirepiox, consisting of 1 carrot, 1 piece celery (chopped rough), and 1 Spanish onion
1 clove garlic, crushed
1 ounce mustard seeds, crushed

4 ounces white wine
2 sprigs fresh thyme
16 ounces demi-glace
2 tablespoons Pommery mustard
Fresh thyme leaves, for garnish
Salt and pepper, to taste

For the red onion marmalade:

2 large red onions, thinly sliced (about 1¼ pounds)
3 tablespoons brown sugar
¾ cup dry red wine

3 tablespoons balsamic vinegar
Salt and pepper, freshly ground, to taste

126

Trim all silverskin from tenderloins; reserve. Preheat oven to 400°F. Place skillet (ovenproof) on high heat; add salt, pepper, and oil. Sear pork on all sides, turning to obtain a golden brown look. Place in oven and let roast until firm to the touch. Remove from oven and let rest for 5 minutes before carving. Cover with aluminum foil. Meat should be slightly pink.

Sauce

Sear pork trimmings in hot oil until brown. Add mirepiox and caramelize. Add garlic and mustard seeds, and cook 5 minutes. Then, deglaze with white wine and add thyme. Reduce until almost dry. Add demi-glace and reduce for 10 minutes. Skim off fat and discard. Strain through fine-mesh strainer into sauce pot. Add Pommery mustard and thyme leaves. Serve with pork tenderloin.

Red Onion Marmalade

In a heavy, large, nonreactive saucepan combine, onions and brown sugar and cook over moderate heat, stirring often until the onions begin to caramelize and turn golden (20 to 25 minutes).

Stir in the wine and vinegar, increase the heat to moderately high, and bring to a boil. Reduce heat to low and cook, stirring often until most of the liquid has evaporated (about 15 minutes).

Season to taste with salt and pepper, and set aside. Serve warm or at room temperature. Can be made 1 week in advance; cover and refrigerate.

To arrange plate:

Slice pork tenderloin on slight bias. Slice thin and let rest on cutting board for 1 minute to allow some of the juices to come out. Place red onion marmalade on plate in center. Fan out sliced pork tenderloin around onions. Ladle sauce around pork. Place a wedge of Julienne Potato Cake (pg. 128) on onions and pork slightly leaning off of them. Garnish with fresh thyme sprig sticking out of onions.

Julienne Potato Cake

Roland Iadanza *(Commack, New York)*

Serves 4 to 6

4 Idaho potatoes, peeled, placed
   in cold water
½ pound clarified butter

4 ounces havarti cheese, grated
Salt and pepper, to taste

Julienne potatoes on a mandoline. Do not soak in water. Dry on a cloth towel. Heat nonstick 8- inch pan. Add butter and heat. Add some of the potatoes on the bottom of the pan, and press down with a spatula. Add cheese on top of potatoes, then add more potatoes on top again with spatula. When potatoes are set, turn or flip them over and place in 400°F oven for 10 minutes. Check for doneness by inserting a small knife or skewer. If it goes through easy, it is done. If you feel the potato breaking as you push through it, it needs more time. Pour off excess butter and let sit for 5 minutes before cutting with a serrated knife. Cut in wedges like a pie and serve.

Shepherd's Pie Using Leg of Lamb Leftovers

Serves 2 to 4

I began making shepherd's pie after the first time I made a leg of lamb. It seemed like the most obvious thing to do. A true shepherd's pie needs to be made with all the leftovers from the leg of lamb dinner the night before, loads of garlic and rosemary, and the leftover gravy, potatoes and vegetables. Here is the very simple version of a lamb pie, as I made it the first time.

1 pound or more leftover lamb
  (or equivalent in cooked lamb,
  diced)
2 tablespoons butter
1 cup carrots, diced

1 cup frozen peas
1½ cups gravy
2 cups mashed potatoes
1 tablespoon parsley
½ tablespoon paprika

Cut up the leftover lamb into bite-size pieces. Mix in your buttered carrots and a cup of frozen peas. Cover with gravy and some water to thin it if necessary. Spread your mashed potatoes over everything. Dot with salted butter. Sprinkle fresh parsley and paprika over potatoes and bake uncovered at 350°F for 45 minutes.

If you don't have enough gravy left over, you can always make a stock with the bone and meat scraps after you've cut off all the chunks of meat for the actual pie, or else use canned beef gravy or a packet of gravy mix.

Beef Shepherd's Pie

Serves 8

I have made this at my cooking demos and it is a big hit, because not everyone likes the gamey flavor of lamb, but they do enjoy the homey shepherd's pie casserole. After making this dish for years, I recently discovered when doing some research that it actually has a name: Cottage Pie. And I thought I had made it up...so much for unique recipes! The beauty of doing cooking demos at local libraries (which I do frequently) is you are cooking for a group of dedicated foodies who are taking notes the whole time, comparing their recipes with mine, and we share tips, quips, and heartfelt stories with each other. I walk around the room with the recipe I am preparing and let the 35 to 50 people see and smell the dish at every stage of preparation close-up. I also pass around whatever herbs I am using so the group can imagine how they will taste in the dish.

5 pounds potatoes

½ stick salted butter

½ cup milk, cream, or half-and-half

½ tablespoon kosher salt

3 pounds lean, chopped sirloin

1 sodium-free packet Herb-Ox® beef bouillon

1 tablespoon extra virgin olive oil

2 yellow onions, sliced small

2 cloves garlic, diced fine

8 sprigs fresh rosemary, leaves removed

½ bunch fresh parsley, chopped fine, stems removed

6 medium to large carrots, peeled, cut into small cubes

1 cup frozen or fresh peas

2 tablespoons cream sherry (more or less depending on your palate)

3 tablespoons dried onion flakes

1 tablespoon powdered garlic

2 tablespoons dried parsley

1 teaspoon paprika

2 tablespoons butter (optional)

Salt, to taste

Gravy

2 to 3½ cups beef stock

1 to 2 tablespoons roux (to thicken stock)

1 tablespoon cream sherry

3 tablespoons teriyaki sauce

2 sprigs fresh rosemary

½ teaspoon garlic powder

1 teaspoon dried onion flakes

1 teaspoon of Gravy Master®

Salt, to taste

Freshly ground pepper, to taste

Prepare mashed potatoes as you normally would, using the potatoes, butter, milk, and salt, and set aside for later use. If you like more butter, add more butter; if you like them creamier, add more milk or cream.

Place meat in skillet, sprinkle with salt and Herb-Ox, and begin to brown. At the halfway point, make a circle in the center of the meat and add 1 tablespoon extra virgin olive oil, then the fresh onion and garlic. Let cook for about 2–3 minutes, and then mix meat, garlic and onion together and fully brown meat. Mix in the rosemary and parsley, and cook 1 minute. Make a circle in center of meat again and add in the carrots. Let them cook on their own for a minute or so, then mix with meat and peas. Mix in the cream sherry well. Layer in the dried onion and garlic. When well mixed and the veggies are beginning to soften, remove from skillet and place into one large or two smaller baking dishes. Set aside.

Make your gravy by adding the stock to a saucepan on a low heat. Add your roux, bring to a gentle boil until desired thickness, keep stirring (do not let it boil over), and add in the sherry, teriyaki, rosemary, garlic, onion, and salt. Keep stirring; when well mixed, let it just come to a gentle boil, then mix in Gravy Master and remove from stove. Pour gravy over prepared meat in baking dishes, just covering completely. Carefully spread the mashed potatoes, using heaping tablespoons, over the meat a section at a time until whole dish is covered. Pat down to smooth into one cohesive layer. Do not let the gravy seep through the potato covering.

Using the prongs of your fork, gently make a design on top either in a series of circles, basketweave, or similar. Dot with butter (if desired). Sprinkle with parsley and paprika, and bake uncovered at 350°F for 35 to 45 minutes until most of the liquid is absorbed. Remove and let set a few minutes before serving. Spoon out over a bed of spinach and serve with Irish soda bread and butter and a healthy helping of a salad of fresh lettuces, spinach, and a dressing of your choice.

Khatta Meetha Chana Masala

Spice Symphony *(Manhattan, New York)*

Serves 4

I recently met up in Manhattan with my best friend of forty years, Terri Fuchs, who was visiting from California. We went on a quest for a great eastern Indian restaurant. I had just attended my neighbor's son's Indian wedding, to which they'd invited our entire cul de sac community, and craved authentic Indian food. We asked a handsome, well-dressed stranger on the street, who turned out to be British, a place famous for Indian food. He directed us to nearby Little India, where we found exactly what we were looking for. This is one of the dishes I'd had at the wedding and was happy to see it on the menu. Tamarind and jaggery give this chana masala a refreshing taste.

1 ½ cups chickpeas (kabuli chana), soaked and boiled
1 tablespoon coriander powder
1 teaspoon cumin powder
1 teaspoon garam masala powder
2 tablespoons chana masala powder
1 teaspoon red chili powder
¼ teaspoon turmeric powder
1 teaspoon amchur powder
2 tablespoons dried pomegranate seeds (anardana)

3 tablespoons ghee
1 teaspoon caraway seeds (shahi jeera)
1 teaspoon cumin seeds
5 green chilies, cut lengthwise
2 tablespoons tamarind pulp
2 tablespoons jaggery (gur)
3 medium tomatoes, chopped
1 cup water
Salt, to taste

Strain chickpeas and reserve the water. Mix together chickpeas, coriander powder, cumin powder, garam masala powder, chana masala powder, red chili powder, turmeric powder, amchur powder, and salt. Dry-roast anardana and grind to a coarse powder. Heat ghee in a nonstick pan, add caraway seeds, cumin seeds, green chillies, and chickpeas, and mix well.

Add anardana powder, tamarind pulp, and jaggery and mix well. Add reserved water, tomatoes, and 1 cup water and cook until the mixture comes to a boil. Transfer into a serving bowl and serve hot.

Palak Paneer Cottage Cheese Cooked in Spinach-Based Gravy

Spice Symphony *(Manhattan, New York)*

Serves 4

> When searching for a great Indian restaurant in Manhattan, we were fortunate enough to take directions from a man in the know, who directed my friend and myself downtown to cuisine nirvana, hidden amid frenzied rush-hour traffic, horns honking, taxis and pedestrians swerving this way and that. This is one of my favorite dishes from its menu and served at almost every Indian meal I have attended, including at my Indian neighbor's wedding party, at which 200 friends and neighbors gathered to celebrate with the young couple.

2 large bunches spinach
2 to 3 green chilies
200 grams paneer (cottage cheese)
8 to 10 cloves garlic

3 tablespoons oil
½ teaspoon cumin seeds
1 tablespoon lemon juice
4 tablespoons fresh cream
Salt, to taste

Remove stems from spinach and wash thoroughly in running water. Blanch in salted, boiling water for 2 minutes. Refresh in chilled water. Squeeze out excess water. Remove stems from green chilies; wash and roughly chop. Grind spinach into a puree along with green chilies. Dice paneer into 1 x 1 x ½-inch pieces. Peel, wash, and chop garlic.

Heat oil in a pan. Add cumin seeds. When they begin to change color, add chopped garlic and sauté for 30 seconds. Add the spinach puree and stir. Check seasoning. Add water if required. When the gravy comes to a boil, add the paneer and mix well. Stir in lemon juice. Finally, add fresh cream. Serve hot.

Dal Makhani with Rajma and Urad Dal

Spice Symphony *(Manhattan, New York)*

Serves 4

Wherever my friend Terri and I go, we find ourselves engaged in meaningful and sometimes hilarious conversation with restaurant staff, as well as the other customers. Very New York of us: we talk to everybody. It really is a small town, to those of us who have grown up here.

I eat everything (in moderation), but Terri has quite a few things she won't eat. She is gluten-free, sugar-free, and mostly vegetarian, so we worry that our dining choices will be limited. Thankfully, our waiters at Spice Symphony are very accommodating, and the owners soon join in explaining every dish on the menu, helping us choose something Terri can eat that will satisfy her food restrictions without skimping on the spicy Indian flavors we crave.

Proprietors Prem and Jude say they would love to place recipes in my book. Everywhere I go, I ask if chefs/cooks would like to share their wonderful dishes with me. Mentioning the big Indian wedding I recently attended, they suggest that this dish could be served at many large gatherings. I recognize it from the wedding and can't wait to make it myself—a very hot and spicy flavor.

½ cup whole black garam (sabut urad)

2 tablespoons red kidney beans (rajma)

6 cups water

1 teaspoon red chili powder

3 tablespoons butter

1 tablespoon oil

1 teaspoon cumin seeds

Ginger, chopped into 2-inch pieces

6 cloves garlic, chopped

1 large onion, chopped

2 green chilies, slit

2 medium tomatoes, chopped

1 teaspoon garam masala powder

Salt, to taste

Pick, wash, and soak sabut urad and rajma overnight in 3 cups of water. Drain. Cook urad and rajma in 3 cups of water with salt and half the red chili powder (you can add half the ginger, too, if you wish). Open the lid and see if the rajma is completely softened. If not, cook on low heat until the rajma becomes completely soft.

Heat butter and oil in a pan. Add cumin seeds. When they begin to change color, add ginger, garlic, and onion and sauté until golden. Add slit green chilies and tomatoes, and sauté on high heat. Add the remaining red chili powder and sauté till the tomatoes are reduced to a pulp. Add the cooked sabat urad and rajma, along with the already cooked mixture. Add some water if the mixture is too thick. Add garam masala powder and adjust salt. Simmer on low heat until the sabat urad and rajma are totally soft and well blended. Serve hot.

Butter Chicken

Spice Symphony Restaurant *(Manhattan, New York)*

Serves 2

Indian wedding ceremonies provide an opportunity for the whole community to celebrate in the pre-wedding blessings and rituals, even before the bride and groom fly off to their destination wedding. At their destination, another 200 to 400 friends and relatives await to attend the actual nuptials. In my community, this brought all of the neighbors even closer than we had been before the event.

The chefs at Spice Symphony supplied me with several dishes that might be served at such a large community gathering or wedding. Though my neighbor's celebratory foods were strictly vegetarian, this chicken dish could be a nice addition to your own community Indian feast. Butter chicken, or *murgh makhani*, is an Indian dish from the Punjab region popular in countries all over the world.

800 grams chicken
1 teaspoon Kashmiri red chili
   powder

1 tablespoon lemon juice
2 tablespoons butter
Salt, to taste

For marinade:

1 teaspoon Kashmiri red chili
   powder
½ teaspoon garlic paste
2 tablespoons ginger paste
2 tablespoons lemon juice
½ teaspoon garam masala
   powder

2 tablespoons cooking oil
1 cup yogurt (Greek, if
   available)
Salt, to taste

For makhni gravy:

50 grams butter
1 tablespoon ginger paste
1 tablespoon garlic paste
4 to 5 green chilies, chopped
400 grams tomato puree
1 tablespoon red chili powder
½ teaspoon garam masala
  powder
2 tablespoons honey (or sugar)

½ teaspoon dry fenugreek
  leaves (kasuri methi)
1 tablespoon whole garam
  masala (green cardamoms,
  cloves, peppercorns and
  cinnamon)
1 cup cream
Salt, to taste

Make incisions with a sharp knife on breast and leg pieces of the chicken. Apply a mixture of red chili powder, lemon juice, and salt to the chicken and set aside for half an hour. For the marinade, add red chili powder, salt, ginger and garlic paste, lemon juice, garam masala powder, and oil to the Greek yogurt.

Apply this marinade to the chicken pieces and refrigerate for 3 to 4 hours. Put the chicken onto a skewer and cook in a moderately hot tandoor or a preheated oven (395°F) for 10 to 12 minutes or until almost done. Baste it with butter and cook for another 2 minutes.

Remove and set aside. Heat butter in a pan. Add whole garam masala (green cardamoms, cloves, peppercorns, and cinnamon). Sauté for 2 minutes; add ginger and garlic paste and chopped green chilies. Cook for 2 minutes. Add tomato puree, red chili powder, garam masala powder, salt, and 1 cup of water. Bring to a boil. Reduce heat and simmer for 10 minutes. Add sugar or honey and powdered kasoori methi. Add cooked tandoori chicken pieces. Simmer for 5 minutes and then add fresh cream. Heat kasoori methi in the oven for some time, or else broil kasoori methi on a tawa/griddle plate to make it crisp. It can easily be crushed into a powder with your hand.

Maple Butter Biscuits

Yields 8 to 10

Biscuits

4½ cups all-purpose flour, plus more for dusting the work surface

1 teaspoon baking soda

1 tablespoon, plus 2 teaspoons baking powder

1 teaspoon salt

2 teaspoons sugar

1 cup solid vegetable shortening

2½ cups buttermilk

Topping

3 tablespoons unsalted butter, cut into small pieces

3 tablespoons maple syrup

¼ teaspoon salt

Biscuits

Preheat oven to 425°F and whisk all of the dry ingredients. Add the vegetable shortening, and with two knives slash across the bowl, cutting the fat into the flour mixture, until it resembles coarse meal with a few large lumps here and there. Add the buttermilk and stir lightly with a rubber spatula just until it comes together. Then, with floured hands, begin kneading the dough until it comes together into a ball. Transfer to a floured surface and knead a little bit more.

Flatten the dough until it is ½ inch thick. Fold it in thirds, then flatten it to ½-inch thickness and fold in thirds again. Repeat several times, then finally flatten the dough to ½ inch thick. Use a floured biscuit cutter to cut out biscuits. Place them on a parchment-lined cookie sheet, and bake for 20 minutes or until the biscuits are golden brown.

Topping

While the biscuits are baking, prepare the maple butter. Bring two tablespoons of water to a boil in a small pot. Slowly whisk in the butter, piece by piece, letting each piece melt before adding the next one. Add the maple syrup and salt and whisk until mixed well. As soon as the biscuits come out of the oven, brush them with the maple butter and serve.

Spicy Two-Bean Vegetarian Chili

Serves 6

2 tablespoons olive oil

1 onion, chopped

2 carrots, peeled, thinly sliced

1 red bell pepper, seeded, chopped

3 large jalapeno chilies, seeded, minced (about 4½ tablespoons)

1 (28-ounce) can crushed tomatoes, with added puree

3 cups water

2 (15-ounce) cans black beans, rinsed, drained

2 (15-ounce) cans kidney beans, rinsed, drained

½ cup bulgur

2 tablespoons white wine vinegar

5 cloves garlic, minced

2 tablespoons chili powder

1½ teaspoons ground cumin

1½ teaspoons ground coriander

½ teaspoon ground cinnamon

Heat 2 tablespoons olive oil in large, heavy pot over medium-high heat. Add onion, carrots, red bell pepper, and jalapeno and sauté until onion and carrots are almost tender (about 8 minutes). Add tomatoes, 3 cups water, beans, bulgur, white wine vinegar, garlic, and spices. Bring to boil. Reduce heat to medium-high and cook, uncovered, until bulgur is tender and mixture thickens, stirring often (about 20 minutes). Ladle chili into bowls and serve.

Baked Stuffed Chicken with Kale and Asparagus

Serves 4

I prepare almost every new dish I create using spinach, asparagus, and, recently, kale. Incorporating them in my recipes helps me to enjoy good food and keep some of the weight off from the not-so-healthy ingredients. This dish was a big hit at my last community cooking demonstration. Doing community cooking demos is really rewarding, because I get to experience a give-and-take with my extremely knowledgeable audience. I've met neighbors, school crossing guards, and even old friends, and find an enriched community spirit every time I do a demo.

6 chicken cutlets, cut thin

Stuffing

1 small package stuffing mix
(follow package directions)
1 onion, diced
1 carrot, diced
¼ cup kale, stems trimmed,
chopped
4 tablespoons butter
1 lemon, juiced and pitted
1 tablespoon capers
⅛ cup cream sherry

⅛ cup half-and-half
1 tablespoon parsley
2 cloves garlic, diced fine
1 yellow onion, diced fine
¼ cup fresh asparagus tips
(microwaved in 1 tablespoon
water for 2 minutes before
adding)
½ tablespoon paprika
Salt and pepper, to taste

Place the chicken cutlets in a baking dish, to be stuffed. To stuff, mix all ingredients (except the paprika) together and spoon 2 to 3 tablespoons into each chicken cutlet, then fold over, placing them seam-side down. Repeat until all cutlets are stuffed.

Any leftover stuffing can be frozen for future use or tucked in around each piece of chicken). Cover and bake 45 minutes. Uncover and sprinkle with paprika and cook an additional 10 minutes.

Part V:

DESSERTS

DESSERTS

"All cakes, over on the left. Cookies and brownies next; then, the pies and trifles." Sound familiar? If it's not the PTA fundraiser for the senior trip, or the baseball team raising money to get to the semifinals, it's the Sunday morning social at the Methodist church. Coveted recipes, which only one person holds the secret to, are swapped and bartered for, as people put their heads together, trying to figure out the secret ingredient behind their neighbor's dessert. Bringing a dessert, whether to sell it for a good cause or share it for fun with friends and neighbors, is one of the sweetest things a person can do.

And it need not be a bake sale; the old-fashioned ice cream social, usually held around summer holidays, gives towns the opportunity to really do it up, decorating to a turn-of-the-century theme. Evoking memories of days gone, people can stroll around on a hot summer day, licking their ice cream cones before they melt. Sail boats race on the bay while kids ride on bikes. A simpler life and simpler time that we all like to wax nostalgic about.

Coyle's Ice Cream in picturesque Brightwaters, New York, draws attention to its town by hosting its annual Fourth of July ice cream social, where the entire community comes out to celebrate the nation's independence together. On any given day, its ice cream parlor will play host to a fundraiser for a local group.

Special treats for special times, each season is dotted with its own reason to stand out, like Potato Chip Sandies (pg. 151) and Old-Fashioned Ginger Snaps (pg. 152). Satisfying our sweet tooth, all while sweetening the relationships within our communities and helping those less fortunate, is what community fundraisers are all about. Raising money, raising awareness, and raising hopes leads to raising a better generation for a better tomorrow.

Cheesecake with Crystallized Ginger

Serves 8

May in the Brooklyn Botanic Garden means the cherry blossoms are in full bloom. The delicate pink flowers contrast with the deep blue of the sky, even as the Japanese Cherry Blossom Festival gets into full swing. Shakuhachi flute music, kabuki, traditional tea ceremonies, and specialty foods are the order of the day. All in all, an event not to be missed; a time when not only the community of Park Slope, but people from all over the city turn out to enjoy themselves. The event itself helps to benefit the upkeep of the Botanic Garden, and enables this Brooklyn oasis to stay open year-round, offering programs for adults and children alike.

This cheesecake is just one of the many treats you may sample. Like so many of the beautiful Japanese scenes you can experience during the festival, this dessert is not only delicious, but stunning to look at with its vibrant colors. The green tea topping evokes all of the new spring growth throughout the garden.

Cheesecake

4 ounces vanilla wafers

2 tablespoons toasted sesame seeds

2 ounces unsalted butter, melted

3½ ounces crystallized ginger, chopped

1 pound cream cheese, softened

⅔ cup confectioner's sugar

1 teaspoon vanilla

1 tablespoon lemon

4 eggs, lightly beaten

Green Tea Topping

2 teaspoons green tea powder

1 tablespoon warm water

1 cup sour cream

½ teaspoon vanilla extract

2 tablespoons confectioner's sugar

146

Line a spring-form, (8-inch) round pan with parchment paper. Crumble the wafers and mix with the sesame seeds. Place in a bowl and add melted butter, stirring to mix completely. Line the bottom of the pan. Chill for 20 minutes, and then layer in the ginger. Beat the cream cheese, sugar, vanilla extract, and lemon juice until smooth. Add the eggs and beat until combined. Do not overbeat, as this may make your cheesecake fall upon cooling. Pour the mixture into the tin and bake for 45 minutes.

For the topping, whisk the powder with 1 tablespoon of warm water until smooth. Then, mix with sour cream, vanilla, and sugar and mix. Spread on the cheesecake while it is still warm and return to the oven to bake for another 7 minutes. Cool on a wire rack for 2 hours, and then chill until firm (about 40 minutes).

Iced Tea Infused with Crystallized Ginger

You can't have cake without a refreshing drink. One of my summer favorites is homemade iced tea. I make many variations, combining different fruit and various teas. Making it yourself affords you the opportunity to control what goes into it. Tea with sugar will never touch my lips. I'm also not too keen on artificially flavored teas, or too many chemical names I can't pronounce, coupled with too many side effects.

The underlying flavor in this particular iced tea is the ginger. For the tea I prefer to use English Breakfast, a favorite of most drinkers. It would also taste great with Earl Grey, chai, or green tea. You can purchase a wide array of dispensers these days, which allows you to dress up any meal or large event with something beautiful, yet functional.

1 gallon dispenser (with spigot)
1 gallon cold filtered water
10 to 12 tea bags (depending on preferred strength)
1 lemon, juiced, pit removed
10 to 12 packets stevia or Truvia® (depending on preferred sweetness)
6 to 8 cubes crystallized ginger

Quick Method

Fill your dispenser with water. Place the tea bags in, with their paper holders anchoring them to the outside of container. Make certain they are all immersed. Stir once or twice. Let sit for at least 30 minutes. Once the tea is dark and strong enough for your taste preference, remove the tea bags and add the juice of one lemon. Stir; add the packets of sweetener, and stir. Add the cubes of ginger. Place in the refrigerator until ready to serve. Add ice to each glass served. Do not add ice to the tea in container, as it will dilute the desired tea flavor.

Longer Method

Place your tea bags in 1 to 2 cups boiled water and allow to steep to desired strength. Fill your gallon container, minus the 1 to 2 cups of hot water. Once you've removed the tea bags from the hot water, add the sweetener to the fully steeped tea and stir to mix. Add this concentrated mixture to the water in your gallon container. Add the juice of 1 lemon and mix; add the crystallized ginger. Place in the refrigerator to chill. It will take a little longer to chill than the quick method. Ideally should be prepared the night before serving for a fully infused, rich flavor. Serve by the glass with ice.

You can infuse your tea (or iced coffee) or plain water with a variety of flavors: whole cloves, cardamom pods, and/or mint, to name a few. Additionally, you can add in slices of fruit from an orange, green apple, honeydew melon, or Bosc pear. Experiment: mix and match both herbs and spices with fruit to infuse an underlying flavor to any iced tea or coffee drink. Nutmeg, cloves, or a cinnamon stick are a good choice for coffee. The items you've chosen to use as an infusion should not be eaten, as all of their flavor will be sapped out. For a large crowd, you can even use several dispensers serving different teas and/or coffees.

Russian Tea Cookies

Kristen Lind *(Sayville, New York)*

Yields 5 dozen

When our town outgrew our library, a new, larger one was built in order to accomodate more computers and work spaces, community meeting spaces and performance rooms, a larger children's section, and just about everything else you could want in a library. Friends of the Library got together to plan several fundraising events, with one such effort resulting in a cookbook, *In the Kitchen with Friends*, filled with recipes like this one from our homey Sayville kitchens.
—*Monica*

1 cup (2 sticks) butter, softened
½ cup confectioner's sugar
1 teaspoon vanilla
2¼ teaspoons vanilla
2¼ cups flour, sifted
¼ teaspoon salt
¾ cup walnuts, finely chopped
1½ cup extra confectioner's sugar for coating

Preheat oven to 400°F. In a large bowl, mix the butter, ½ cup confectioner's sugar, and vanilla. Sift together the sifted flour and salt. Gradually stir into the butter mixture. Stir in the chopped nuts. Form into 1-inch balls. Place 2 inches apart on a parchment paper-lined cookie sheet. Bake for 12 to 14 minutes until very lightly browned.

Gently remove cookies from cookie sheet and place on a cooling rack. Place 1 cup of the extra confectioner's sugar in a large resealable bag. While still warm, place a few cookies at a time in the bag and gently roll the cookies in confectioner's sugar. Let cool somewhat and repeat the process to coat again with the remaining ½ cup of the extra confectioner's sugar, until all cookies are coated.

Potato Chip Sandies

Ethelinda J. Ellis *(Sayville, NY)*

When the new, three-story library was completed in our town and was ready for its grand opening, newly published cookbooks were on hand for purchase to continue to build upon the continued fundraising efforts. Now the library system is celebrating 100 years of operations, and a year's worth of festivities are ongoing, including sales of its popular cookbook. Cookies and milk are still a favorite after-school snack, and parents are always looking for a new recipe to wow the kids or to donate to the school's fundraising bake sales. They have just the right mix of salty and sweet.
—*Monica*

1 cup butter
½ cup sugar
1 teaspoon vanilla extract
½ cup potato chips, crushed

½ cup pecans, chopped
2 cups flour
Extra sugar for flattening

Preheat oven to 325°F. Cream butter and sugar. Add vanilla. Add potato chips and pecans. Stir in flour. Form balls of dough (approximately 1 tablespooon each). Press balls flat with the bottom of a glass dipped in sugar. Bake for approximately 8 minutes. Cook on a baker's rack.

COUNTRY COMFORT: POTLUCK FAVORITES

Old-Fashioned Ginger Snaps

Kristen Lind *(Sayville, New York)*

Kristen is on the committee for her local Friends of the Library, and has also spent years doing countless fundraisers for her local schools: bake sales, art shows, raffles—all benefiting the children of her community. Her forte is baking, and this recipe will take you right back to the scents of your grandmother's kitchen. Kristen often gets her eggs from her neighbor, who keeps lovely chickens in her bucolic suburban yard: a throwback to a simpler time.

—*Monica*

¾ cups butter

1 cup sugar, plus extra sugar
   for rolling

4 tablespoons molasses

1 large egg

2 cups flour, sifted

2 teaspoons baking soda

1 teaspoon cinnamon

¾ teaspoon ground cloves

1 teaspoon ginger

¼ teaspoon allspice

Preheat oven to 350°F. In a large bowl, cream butter and sugar. Add molasses and egg to butter mixture and mix until smooth. In a separate bowl, combine the flour, baking soda, cinnamon, cloves, ginger, and allspice. Mix well. Add the flour mixture to the wet ingredients and stir. Roll into small balls and roll into sugar. Place on a parchment paper-lined baking sheet and bake for 12 minutes. Remove from oven and let rest on cookie sheet for 2 minutes. Remove to a cooling rack.

Peanut Butter Cookies

Stephanie Devery *(Oakdale, New York)*

Yields 2 to 3 dozen

> These cookies are a take on the classic peanut butter cookie. Instead of using a chocolate kiss on top, they are lined with mini chocolate chips: a real crowd pleaser.

2½ cups all-purpose flour
1 teaspoon baking powder
1 teaspoon baking soda
½ teaspoon salt
1 cup butter, softened
1 cup creamy peanut butter
1 cup sugar

1 cup light brown sugar, firmly
    packed
2 eggs
1 teaspoon vanilla
12-ounce bag mini semisweet
    chocolate chips

Preheat oven to 350°F. Mix together the flour, baking powder, baking soda, and salt in a small bowl. In a large bowl, beat the butter and peanut butter until smooth. Beat in sugars until well blended. Beat in the eggs one at a time and add vanilla. Add the flour mixture; beat until well blended. Chill the dough for 2 hours. Shape into 1-inch balls. Place 2 inches apart on ungreased cookie sheets. Bake for 12 minutes, or until lightly browned.

Remove cookies from cookie sheet immediately and place onto cooling rack. Place mini chocolate chips around edges of the cookies. Let cool completely; it will be about 3 hours until the chocolate hardens.

Kris's Oatmeal Berry Cherry Cookies

Kristen Lind *(Sayville, New York)*

Yields 4 dozen

When the new library opened in Kristen's town, it was a grand community affair. Many of the recipes like this one from its *The Friends of the Library* cookbook were served at the reception and were very well received. To this day, the book is sold at the front counter in a continued fundraising effort.
—*Monica*

½ pound (2 sticks) butter, softened
1 cup brown sugar, firmly packed
½ cup granulated sugar
2 large eggs
1 teaspoon vanilla extract
1½ cups all-purpose flour
1 teaspoon baking soda

1 teaspoon cinnamon
½ teaspoon salt
3 cups Quaker™ Old Fashioned Oats, uncooked
1 cup dried blueberries (sweetened)
1 cup dried cherries (sweetened) or 1 cup dried cranberries

Preheat oven to 350°F. In a large mixing bowl, beat together the butter and sugars until creamy. Add eggs and vanilla and beat well. Combine flour, baking soda, cinnamon, and salt. Mix well. Add the flour mixture to the wet ingredients and stir. Stir in the oats, blueberries, and cherries. Drop by rounded tablespoon on parchment paper-lined cookie sheet, keeping cookies 2 inches apart. Bake 10 to 12 minutes or until golden brown. Cool 1 minute on cookie sheet. Remove to a wire rack.

Mock Zeppoles

Susan and Ronnie Grant *(Sayville, New York)*

Serves 6

I recently had the opportunity to visit my friends Sue and Ronnie in their home in Bethel, New York. If the name is familiar to anyone, that is because the town is the original site of the historically significant Woodstock Festival. An otherwise sleepy town tucked into the Catskills back in the 1960s, Bethel Woods has transformed over the years into a mecca for music lovers, boasting outdoor concerts serving local foods and craft brews, a museum, and beautiful meditative grounds where one can visit, imagining for a moment that they'd been there back in the day. Sue shared one of Ronnie's mom's secret recipes for a decadent dessert: mock zeppoles. You can't eat more than two, but you must have at least one.

—*Monica*

2 cups vegetable oil
1 tube biscuit dough
12 marshmallows

1 cup confectioner's sugar
1 large plastic food-storage bag

Heat vegetable oil in a medium saucepan. Separate the twelve biscuits and, one at a time, press to spread. Spread thin, simply using your hands. Place a marshmallow in the center of each one and pull up the sides to completely cover the entire marshmallow, sealing any openings. Roll into a ball. Drop one at a time into the hot oil (up to three at a time in the pot) and cook for about 1 minute, or until the balls are lightly golden brown on all sides. Remove with a slotted spoon and drain on paper towels. Continue until all twelve are done. Place several at a time in the bag filled with confectioner's sugar and shake to coat. Eat immediately while still warm.

Variations

I thought I'd discovered gold when I learned how to do this. My mind raced and thought instantly of jelly doughnuts, using a teaspoonful of preserves in the center instead of the marshmallow. A chocolate kiss, or even nothing inside, instead coated with brown sugar and cinnamon. For the lovers of a savory treat, a piece of cheese and scallion or sour cream and chives, coated with a mélange of your favorite spices, herbs, and a little salt and pepper. The possibilities are endless.

Streusel

Harry Myers *(Lipan, Texas)*

Serves 8

At any large gathering, whether to commemorate an event or just to share homemade treats, the dessert is always anticipated. The variety is endless, and includes pies, of course. Pie crusts are an art in itself. My favorite topping is a flavorful crumb, or streusel, as at is called. We are all familiar with its variations, ranging from Dutch apple pie to coffee cakes to name a few. There are many different recipes for streusel. My favorite, which is perfect for pies and cakes, always pleases the streusel aficionados.

1 stick unsalted butter, melted	2 teaspoons ground cinnamon
½ cup white sugar	½ teaspoon salt
1 cup all-purpose flour	1 teaspoon vanilla extract

Blend the ingredients in a medium bowl with a fork until large crumbs appear. Squeeze the powdery residue with your fingers to form additional lumps. Refrigerate for 20 minutes to harden the crumbs for sprinkling. When cooled, break up crumbs into about the size of raisins and marbles with your fork. Use your fingers to form the smaller ones into little balls. Spread over pie or cake, and press lightly not to crush the crumbs.

To avoid hard caramelized crumbs, bake uncovered for 20 to 25 minutes at 350 to 425°F, and then cover with aluminum foil for remainder of baking, which is not to exceed 45 minutes. Check topping after 35 minutes and make sure it isn't getting burned on the top. It should be a light tan color. Leave the foil on top of the finished cake or pie to retain moisture and keep the topping slightly moist until cooled. There should be a little moisture on the foil bottom. There will be a little trial and error before you can get it to your liking, but once you get it the way you prefer, it will be your signature streusel.

The vanilla can be substituted with other flavor extracts, such as coconut, almond, lemon, etc. I do not recommend using brown sugar, as it contains molasses, which tends to caramelize and become hard and difficult to chew. Most people like crumb topping to be soft, with a hint of crunch.

Lemon Pound Cake

Marie Mandell *(Sayville, New York)*

Serves 12

2¼ cups all-purpose flour
2 cups sugar
½ teaspoon salt
½ teaspoon baking soda
1 teaspoon grated lemon peel
1 teaspoon vanilla extract

1 cup butter, softened
1 container (8 ounces) sour
   cream
3 eggs
1 cup confectioner's sugar
1 to 2 tablespoons lemon juice

Preheat oven to 325°F. Grease and flour 12-cup (10-inch-high) Bundt or tube pan. In a large bowl using an electric mixer, combine flour, sugar, salt, baking soda, lemon peel, vanilla, butter, sour cream, and eggs. Blend at low speed. Beat for 3 minutes at medium speed and pour batter in prepared pan. Bake for 60 to 70 minutes, or until top of cake springs back when touched in the center. Cool cake for 15 minutes. Remove cake from pan. Blend confectioner's sugar and lemon juice to a pouring consistency. Pour over cooled cake.

Warm Apple Tart with Bourbon Pecan Crème Anglaise

Roland Iadanza *(Commack, New York)*

Serves 4; yields 2 tarts

Apple Tart

1 sheet of puff pastry
2 large Golden Delicious apples, peeled, cored, and sliced thin
1½ tablespoons melted butter
1 tablespoon sugar
1 tablespoon confectioner's sugar

½ teaspoon ground cinnamon
8 ounce pecans, chopped for garnish
Mint leaf, for garnish

Crème Anglaise

16 ounces milk
4 ounces sugar
½ vanilla bean split

4 egg yolks
½ ounce Wild Turkey bourbon

Apple Tart

Thaw pastry for 20 minutes. Unfold and roll on a lightly floured surface to a 12 x 9-inch rectangle. Cut out two 6-inch circles and place on ungreased baking sheet. Arrange apples on top in a spiral fashion, brush with butter, and sprinkle with a mixture of the two sugars and cinnamon. Bake at 325°F for 35 to 40 minutes.

Crème Anglaise

Bring milk, sugar, and vanilla bean to a boil. Whip egg yolks; add a little of the hot milk mixture to egg yolks until half of the milk is in. Pour back into sauce pot over medium-high heat. Stir until mixture coats the back of a spoon. Do not boil. Add Wild Turkey. Strain through fine strainer. Let cool. To serve, place a pool of the crème anglaise in center of the plate. Place warm apple tart in middle of sauce. Garnish with chopped pecans and dust edges of place with cinnamon and powdered sugar. Garnish with mint leaf. Serve.

Harry's Donuts

Harry Myers *(Lipan, Texas)*

Yields 2 dozen donuts

> While most people bring a cake or cookies to a community pot-luck, Harry outdoes himself and brings two dozen homemade donuts. He is a real risk taker, and chooses treats others would be afraid to even attempt. They are always the first to go at an event. (In fact, after hearing about the success of his baking endeavors, I just may have to move to Texas to experience all the great food Harry has to offer.)

1 tablespoon fast active yeast
(with ¼ teaspoon sugar to
speed yeast)
1 cup sugar
¾ cup warm water
¾ warm milk

4 cups all-purpose flour
1 teaspoon vanilla extract
2 teaspoon salt
2 tablespoon soft butter
1 egg

Heat oil to 375°F. In a mixing bowl, add yeast, sugar, water and milk. Mix and wait for yeast to foam (about 10 minutes). Add flour, sugar, vanilla, salt, butter, and egg. Next, mix with kneading hook in stand mixer for 6 minutes until sides of bowl are clean, and dough becomes a soft ball. Place pliable dough in lightly oiled bowl to coat both sides of dough and cover until doubled in size (1 hour or more).

Punch down and roll out sheet ¾ thick and cut with 3-inch round cutter. Punch center hole with open pill bottle and save the pieces. Place donuts on pan to rise for another hour or more until light and fluffy. Lift donuts off carefully to avoid deflating, place in basket without crowding, and fry each side until golden brown, but not dark, or donuts will not be soft. Drop in "holes" after donuts are made. Do not overcook. Place on paper towels to absorb excess oil.

Sprinkle with powdered sugar, or dip in frosting of your choice.

To make glaze: in bowl take 2 cups powdered sugar, 1 teaspoon vanilla extract, 3 or more tablespoons of water, and mix to thin consistency. Dip donuts, and let glaze dry to transparent film.

Brownie Chocolate Chip Cookies

Stephanie Devery *(Oakdale, New York)*

Makes 3 dozen

> These amazing cookies are a cross between a brownie and a chocolate chip cookie. They have the chewy consistency of a brownie combined with the crispiness of a chocolate chip cookie. Delicious!

8 ounce semisweet chocolate, chopped
8 ounce unsweetened chocolate, chopped
4 tablespoons unsalted butter
½ cup all-purpose flour
½ teaspoon baking powder
½ teaspoon salt
4 large eggs, room temperature
1½ cups sugar
1 teaspoon pure vanilla extract
1 (12-ounce) bag semisweet chocolate chips

Preheat the oven to 350°F and line two baking sheets with parchment paper. In a large bowl over a double boiler, melt the chopped chocolate with the butter, stirring a few times, until smooth, and completely melted. In a small bowl, combine flour, baking powder and salt.

In another large bowl, using a handheld electric mixer, beat the eggs with the sugar at medium speed until thick and pale in color. Beat in the vanilla extract. Fold in all of the melted chocolate; mix until combined. Then stir in the flour mixture. Stir in the chocolate chips. All should be well combined.

Place two tablespoon-size pats of dough onto the prepared sheets, about 2 inches apart. Bake for about 10 minutes, until the cookies are firm and dry around the edges. Let the cookies cool on the baking sheets for 10 minutes, then transfer to a rack and cool completely before serving.

Frozen Peanut Butter Candy Pie

Stefanie Devery *(Oakdale, New York)*

Yields 8

This recipe is fabulous for a barbecue or party. You can prepare it the day before; everyone loves candy and peanut butter! (It is also a "no bake" pie).

8 ounce cream cheese, room temperature
¾ cup confectioner's sugar
½ cup crunchy peanut butter
2 tablespoons milk

½ cup roasted peanuts, chopped
2 cups heavy cream, whipped until thick
1 (9-inch) graham cracker crust
1 cup chocolate sauce

Toppings (see Tip below)

Using a stand mixer fitted with the whip attachment, beat the cream cheese and sugar until they are smooth. Add the peanut butter, milk, and roasted peanuts and beat well. Fold 2 cups of the whipped heavy cream into the cheese mixture. Pour the filling into the prepared crust. Cover the entire top of the pie with the (see *Tip* below). Place in the freezer for a minimum of 4 hours, preferably overnight.

About 10 minutes before serving, take pie out of the freezer and drizzle chocolate sauce over the top.

A handful of each of the following makes for an easy, yet varied topping bar: M&M'S®, Snickers® (chopped), Heath Bar (chopped), Reese's Pieces, and/or Reese's Peanut Butter Cups (chopped).

Jewish Apple Cake

Stefanie Devery *(Oakdale, New York)*

Serves 6

> This cake is a favorite at my house for Rosh Hashanah. Apples are used to represent a sweet New Year. This cake is moist and flavorful with a hint of cinnamon.

5 apples, mix of Granny Smith and Gala
2 teaspoons cinnamon
2½ cups sugar
3 cups sifted all-purpose flour
3 teaspoons baking powder
½ teaspoon salt
1 cup butter
4 eggs
⅓ cup orange juice
1½ teaspoons pure vanilla extract
1 teaspoon almond extract
Confectioners' sugar, if desired for topping cake

Preheat oven to 350°F. Grease and flour a 10-inch tube pan. Set aside. Peel and quarter apples, then core and slice them. In a small mixing bowl, combine apples, cinnamon, and ½ cup of the sugar. Coat the apples well. In a small mixing bowl, combine the flour, baking powder, and salt. Set aside.

In a large mixing bowl, using an electric mixer, cream the butter and 2 cups of the sugar until fluffy. Add the eggs, one at a time, mixing well after each addition. Add the flour mixture to the butter mixture. Combine well. Add the juice and the extracts. Continue mixing the batter until batter is smooth.

Place a small amount of batter on the bottom of the pan. Arrange a layer of apple slices, then add more batter over the apples; continue layering with batter and apples, ending with batter. Bake for 1½ hours. Cool on wire rack. Dust with confectioner's sugar, if desired.

Chocolate Zucchini Bread

North Fork Bed and Breakfast Association *(Long Island, New York)*

Courtesy of Mark MacNish, Andrew's Legacy BandB *(Cutchogue, New York)*

Arbor View Bed and Breakfast, Veda Joseph *(East Marion, New York)*

Serves 8

2½ cups all-purpose flour
2 cups sugar
1 teaspoon salt
1 teaspoon ground cinnamon
2 teaspoons baking soda
¼ teaspoon baking powder
½ cup unsweetened cocoa
  powder

½ cup chopped walnuts
½ cup choclate chips
3 large eggs
1 cup vegetable oil
2 teaspoons vanilla extract
3 cups unpeeled zucchini,
  grated

Preheat oven to 350°F. Combine flour, sugar, salt, cinnamon, baking soda, baking powder, cocoa, walnuts, and chocolate chips in a large bowl. In a medium bowl, whisk eggs slightly, then whisk in oil and vanilla. Stir in zucchini, add mixture to dry ingredients, and mix thoroughly. Pour into two loaf pans lightly sprayed with cooking spray. Bake until a toothpick comes out clean (50 to 55 minutes). Cool 10 minutes on baker's rack. Run a knife around edges to remove from pan. When cooled, wrap in aluminum foil.

The Versatile Tart

North Fork Bed and Breakfast Association *(Long Island, New York)*

Courtesy of Mark MacNish

Serves 8

I remember the first time I went into a high-end bakery and saw a raspberry tart in the display case. It was judiciously sprinkled with powdered sugar, and fresh raspberries were arranged in a neat concentric circle, contained by a sweet crust perimeter that looked like a miniature landscape fence.

How elegant it looked. It stood out next to the other baked goods. Its high cost also helped to set it apart, so I assumed it was difficult to make, and from what I understood, I was not alone in this assumption. But once you have tart pans and pie weights (a pound of dried beans could substitute for these), making a tart turns out not to be that difficult at all.

The basic sweet tart crust can be used with all sorts of fruits and can serve as the standard for you to use with different fruits as they come into season. A sweet fruit tart consists of the crust and a layer of jam or preserves, and is topped off by the fresh fruit, being served with whipped cream, ice cream, or crème fraîche. Raspberries go over raspberry jam, strawberries over strawberry jam, and so on. This recipe makes enough for a 10-inch round pan and can be adjusted accordingly to pan size and type.

¼ cup unsalted butter (at room temperature)
½ teaspoon vanilla extract
½ cup sugar

1 ⅓ cups all-purpose flour
¼ teaspoon salt
1 cup preserves (optional)
Powdered sugar (optional)

Preheat oven to 350°F. With a wooden spoon, mix the butter, vanilla, and sugar together. In a separate bowl sift the flour and salt and add the butter mixture; mix on low speed until it starts to form a dough. Put dough into a 10-inch tart pan and press the dough evenly over the bottom and up the sides, making sure the finished edge is flat. Chill until firm. Grease one side of a rounded piece of aluminum foil to fit the tart. Place it greased-side down, on the dough. Fill with pie weights or beans. Bake for about 20 to 25 minutes until lightly brown. Allow to cool and remove from tart pan. Spread with about a cup of preserves or jam and arrange about a pint and a half of fruit on top. Sprinkle with powdered sugar if desired. Serve soon.

White Chocolate Peppermint Drops

Stefanie Devery *(Oakdale, New York)*

Yields approximately 80 cookies

> These cookies look amazing on your holiday table. The red and white of the crushed peppermint on top of the cookie is so festive.

1½ cups butter, softened
1 cup sugar
1 teaspoon baking powder
1 egg
1 teaspoon peppermint extract
3½ cups all-purpose flour

6 ounces white chocolate chips
1 tablespoon shortening
1 (12-ounce) bag peppermint candies, finely crushed
Red food coloring, if desired

Preheat oven to 375°F. In a large bowl, beat butter and sugar with an electric mixer on medium speed until soft. Add the baking powder and beat until creamy and lighter in color. Add egg and peppermint extract. Beat in the flour in three equal amounts until combined. Add about 7 to 10 drops of the food coloring, if desired.

Roll 1-inch balls of the unchilled cookie dough. Place on a parchment-lined cookie sheet. Bake for 8 to 10 minutes, until cookies are firm, but not browned. Cool completely. Once cookies are cool, prepare the white chocolate. Over a double boiler, melt the white chocolate chips with shortening. Dip the tops of each cookie in the white chocolate, and then dip into the crushed peppermint candies.

Proper English Trifle

Serves 8 to 12

Although this is a proper English trifle, it is also a popular dessert at any Saint Patrick's Day celebration. Before beginning to build your trifle and make the pudding, freeze your pound cake overnight. This makes for easier cutting and shaping. Try to let all of your layers show through the glass independently and not meld into each other. When I presented this at one of my library food demos, I strived to be as authentic as possible with my ingredients and presentation. I had feared that people may not like the homemade custard as much as the instant pudding mixes, which so many people have become used to, but happily most in the audience enjoyed them equally as much.

Pound Cake

1 pound cake

⅓ cup cream sherry

½ cup raspberry preserves

4 cups berries (strawberries or blueberries)

2 kiwi fruits, peeled and cut into chunks

2 fresh peaches, peeled, pitted, cut into chunks

Custard

2 cups milk

8 egg yolks

1¼ cups sugar

1 teaspoon vanilla extract

Whipped Cream Topping

½ pint whipping cream

2 tablespoons powdered sugar

Sliced strawberries, for topping

Crumbled nuts, for topping (optional)

Pound Cake

Make pound cake and freeze overnight. Cut pound cake in half (lengthwise) and place as your first layer in trifle. You may have to trim it a bit to fit properly. Fill in empty spots. Brush cake with sherry, and then spread with the preserves. Place a layer of strawberries, a layer of blueberries (and a layer of any other berries you may be using). Place a layer of kiwi. Place a layer of peaches.

Custard

Heat milk in the top of a double boiler until a film forms on the top. Beat eggs with sugar and vanilla in another double boiler until it forms a ribbon. Very slowly pour the heated milk into the egg mixture, beating constantly. Place the entire mixture into another saucepan and stir over low heat until the custard thickens (about 15 to 20 minutes). Do *not* let it boil. Remove and cool in a bowl of ice water, stirring occasionally, careful not to let water infiltrate pudding.

Once cooled, spoon over the fruit in trifle dish. Cover and refrigerate overnight (or at least 6 hours before serving). Right before serving, whip cream using the whipping cream and powdered sugar. Spoon over the prepared trifle and spread evenly. Decorate the top with sliced strawberries (and nuts if desired).

Chef's Tips

Before your meal ever reaches the table, there are many steps that have gone into making it the best dish ever. That tender, juicy chicken, or those ribs that seem to melt off the bone, even the fish, just caught and grilled to perfection, are all the end result of skill and experience on the part of the chef. The secret is often a combination of fresh ingredients, ideally homegrown or farmed locally, coupled with the creative manipulations of herbs, spices, vinegars, and oils.

I've shared some of these clever ideas with you here; whether you use it cooking for your family of four or a family of friends at your next community get-together, you will be able to bring your dishes to the next level. Take extra time to know where your food comes from and get in the habit of using the freshest ingredients possible.

Brines, Rubs, and Marinades

A **brine** enables you to infuse flavors right to the bone, before you've even begun to actually grill or bake your meats. It holds the moisture within the meat, all while picking up the subtle flavors of the brine. With a brine, you will want to treat your meats overnight in the refrigerator. For large amounts, you will need room for a big tub or canister, as the meat needs to be fully submerged. Before cooking, dry off the meat completely.

A **rub** will help to tenderize a tougher cut of beef or a rack of ribs while adding flavor topically. This is great for grilled foods, keeping them moister inside. A dry rub can be applied as little as half an hour in advance for a taste difference, and can be your opportunity to add a spicy kick or a smoky flavor. Adding a little oil, vinegar, or fruit juice will moisten your rub for better application.

A **marinade** also serves to tenderize, but unlike the rub, a marinade permeates the meat throughout. You can marinate in the refrigerator from 1 hour to overnight, shaking or turning to cover all sides before cooking in the oven or on the grill. When grilling, many will discard the marinade, but in truth you can apply it throughout the grilling process, brushing it on as the meat cooks. Be careful *not* to use the marinade during the last several minutes of your cooking; due to the raw meat, you won't have enough time to cook it off properly. Using fruit in your marinade can form a delicious crispy or carmelized coating on your meat. One last thing: give yourself enough time at the end, and *never* pour the marinade over the cooked meat at table.

Brine for Pork or Turkey

Roland Iadanza

1 ½ gallons water
½ cup kosher salt
½ cup dried thyme
½ cup juniper berry

½ cup black peppercorns
4 bay leaves
¼ cup sugar

Place all ingredients in large pot and bring to one boil only. Do not simmer, or the brine will be too strong. Cool and place in container large enough to submerge the entire item. Add pork loin or turkey to cool brine for 24 hours. A brining bag may be used. Pat dry and roast. This creates a moist, juicy product.

Brine for Chicken

1 ½ gallons water
⅓ cup kosher salt
1 cup brown sugar

½ cup Vermont maple syrup
½ cup cloves

Follow method above for pork or turkey to prepare a brine for chicken.

Brine to Smoke a Ham

30 grams of sea salt, finely
   ground
2 ½ grams of curing salt
5 grams muscovade sugar
¼ teaspoon ground allspice

¼ teaspoon ground cardamom
¼ teaspoon ground cloves
⅛ teaspoon ground black
   pepper

Follow method above for pork or turkey to prepare a brine for smoking ham.

Drying Fresh Caught Salmon

Hank Shaw

Salmon, particularly smoked salmon, is a perfect seafood dish to complement a big summer cookout. Light and flaky, with flavor ranging from mild to strong, salmon is ideal to serve to large numbers of people, of varying tastes and palates.

Brine for Smoked Salmon

Makes enough brine for 5 pounds of fish

Prep Time: 24 hours (including refrigeration)
Cook Time: 6 hours (depending on temperature and preference)

5 pounds salmon, trout, or char
1 quart cool water
⅓ cup kosher salt
1 cup brown sugar
½ cup birch syrup or maple syrup
Birch or maple syrup, for basting

Mix together brine ingredients and place in a plastic or glass (non-reactive container). Cover and refrigerate. Cure thin filets at least 8 hours; larger, thicker pieces could go as long as 36 hours. Don't go over 48 hours or the fish will be too salty.

New Orleans Dry Rub

2½ tablespoons paprika
2 tablespoons salt
2 tablespoons garlic powder
1 tablespoon black pepper

1 tablespoon onion powder
1 tablespoon cayenne pepper
1 tablespoon dried oregano
1 tablespoon dried thyme

Rub ingredients into the meat thoroughly, coating grill with olive oil and grilling to your desired doneness.

Texas-Style Dry Rub

2 tablespoons salt
1 tablespoon pepper

½ tablespoon garlic powder
1 tablespoon brown sugar

For Mexican influence add:
1 tablespoon chili powder
1 teaspoon cumin

½ teaspoon cayene pepper

For savory influence add:
1 tablespoon onion powder
1 teaspoon dried thyme

1 teaspoon dried rosemary
¼ teaspoon paprika

For Asian influence add:
1 tablespoon onion powder
1½ tablespoons ground ginger

½ teaspoon wasabi

For East Indian add:
1 teaspoon ground coriander
1 teaspoon ground cardamom

1 teaspoon dried fennel
1 teaspoon yellow curry powder

For each alternative, rub into the meat thoroughly, coat grill with olive oil, and grill to your desired doneness. The brown sugar will help carmelize the meat.

Asian-Influenced Marinade

1 cup soy sauce
1 cup mirin
1 cup sake
4 tablespoons stevia, sugar, or
   honey

1 inch ginger, peeled and grated
¼ cup sesame seeds

Boil all ingredients for about a minute (except the sesame seeds). Once removed from the heat, add in the sesame seeds. Allow it to cool before placing meat in. Refrigerate the marinating meat for at least ½ hour (and up to 4 hours).

Italian-Influenced Marinade

½ cup water
½ cup white balsamic vinegar
⅓ cup extra virgin olive oil
6 cloves garlic, pressed
½ teaspoon oregano
½ teaspoon parsley

1 teaspoon thyme
1 teaspoon rosemary
1 teaspoon salt
1 teaspoon freshly ground
   peppercorns (mixed color)

Mix all ingredients. Marinate over meat in a plastic bag or casserole dish in the refrigerator from ½ hour to 4 hours. Then, grill or bake.

Making a Roux

Chef John B.

A roux is a classically used thickening agent, useful in preparing any number of soups and sauces. Created by adding equal parts flour to fat (this can be substituted for other, similarly thickening ingredients), a roux is one of the staples in French cuisine. An easy way to create a roux (healthier than using bacon grease or similar fats) is by combining 2 tablespoons of flour and 2 tablespoons of butter (or, if more is needed, use 1 cup of flour to 1 cup of butter or oil). Cook about 5 minutes (be sure not to overcook; color should be blonde). Add 2 tablespoons of stock to smooth consistency, and add to recipe. Rule of thumb: use about 1 tablespoon of roux to every 1½ cups of stock.

Thickener Equivalents		
1½ teaspoons arrowroot	=	1 tablespoon flour plus 1½ teaspoons cornstarch
1 tablespoon cornstarch	=	2 tablespoons all-purpose flour plus 2 tablespoons granular tapioca
1 tablespoon all-purpose flour (exclusively for thickening)	=	any of these choices: 1½ teaspoons cornstarch, arrowroot starch, potato starch, or rice starch; 1 tablespoon granular tapioca; 1 tablespoon waxy rice flour; 2 tablespoons browned flour; or 1½ tablespoons whole wheat flour
1 tablespoon granular tapioca	=	2 tablespoons pearl tapioca

Drying Fruit

Successfully drying fruit depends on heat, air dryness, and good air circulation. Select fresh, fully ripened fruits. Thoroughly wash, sort through, and discard any fruit that shows decay, bruising, or mold. Pretreat each fruit piece by dipping in lemon juice. When dry, allow fruit to condition for 4 to 10 days, before packaging for storage. Package dried fruits in tightly sealed containers and store in a cool, dry place. Dried fruit makes for a great snack, but an even better addition to any number of desserts, salads, and entrées, ensuring that your dish is well received at your next community event.

Growing Your Own Food

Healthy living does not mean giving up good food and great flavor. Simply eating unprocessed food and employing healthy cooking methods will put you on track for better overall health. Serving fresh garlic, green, leafy vegetables like spinach and kale, herbs like basil and parsley, and using extra virgin olive oil for sauteeing and salad dressings are all great ways to improve and maintain a healthier lifestyle.

Growing some of your own vegetables and fruits has the added benefits of saving money and increasing quality family time by working together in the garden. Blueberries and raspberries are easy to grow, and can be great options for beginning gardeners.

Monica's Italian garden is comprised of herbs such as oregano, basil, and parsley, along with cherry, plum, and beefsteak tomatoes, eggplant, green and red peppers, and zucchini. Harvest the peppers, eggplant, tomatoes, and zucchini through mid-autumn. She also grows broccoli, cucumber, lettuce, and additional herbs, including mint, chives, sage, dill, rosemary, cilantro (which, when it goes to seed, results in coriander), and lavender. We eat what is most plentiful as it is picked, and then prepare and freeze the rest for future use.

It is important to pick at just the right time to elicit the maximum flavor, texture, and nutritional value. You can get the most vitamins and minerals from your produce by using them as soon after harvesting as possible. Essential vitamins and minerals enable our bodies to function properly, which helps us to live longer, more productive lives. It is also important to store your precious fruits and vegetables properly, being careful not to bruise them while picking, because they will spoil more quickly.

Resources

Chef Maureen Denning
www.thesnapperinn.com

Stefanie Devery
www.butterandbliss.com
Twitter: @ButterandBliss
Facebook: https://www.facebook.com/butterandbliss

Ron Gelish
www.hc.saladmaster.com
hc.saladmaster@gmail.com

Chef Roland Iadanza, Territory Sales Manager
RC Fine Foods, Suffolk County, NY
iadanza11@yahoo.com

Jaclyn L. Messina
Jac's Bakeshop & Bistro: Long Island's Completely Gluten Free Bakery
www.jacsbakeshopandbistro.com
Facebook: www.facebook.com/Jacsbakeshop

Chef Chris Lang, Director, Culinary Services
Atria Tanglewood
christopher.lang@atriaseniorliving.com

Harry I. Myers
info@poochkies.com

Hank Shaw, Hunter, Angler, Gardener, and Cook
Author of *Hunt, Gather, Cook: Finding the Forgotten Feast* (Rodale 2011) and *Duck, Duck, Goose: Recipes and Techniques for Cooking Ducks and Geese* (Ten Speed 2013)
scrbblr@hotmail.com

Spice Symphony
www.spicesymphony.com
spicesymphony@gmail.comhide
premchouhan1969@gmail.com

Helpful Websites

Epicurious
www.epicurious.com

Food Network
www.foodnetwork.com

Allrecipes.com
www.allrecipes.com

Taste of Home
www.tasteofhome.com

Simply Recipes
www.simplyrecipes.com

eHow
www.ehow.com

About the Author

Monica Musetti-Carlin holds a degree in liberal arts and is an award-winning media consultant for a chain of newspapers on Long Island. As a journalist, lecturer, and "foodie" with over 30 years of experience in media, she continues to publish news and feature stories, advertorials, restaurant reviews, recipes, advertising, copywriting, and public relations pieces for such publications as the *New York Times*, *New York Magazine*, and many New York weeklies. Through her advertising agency, Monica Musetti Advertising, Marketing, Promotion, Special Events, and Public Relations, she has had the opportunity to work with Jane Brody, Pete Seeger, and Yoko Ono. Most recently, in addition to writing the Country Comfort series, she is completing several nonfiction and fictional works in progress and is expanding her Special Events division, Eclectic Endeavors, to enhance the marketing and distribution of her recipe and craft product lines.

Dedication

This book is dedicated to my son Matthew Carlin who has stood beside me helping out at so many of the events I have had the pleasure of running. And, to all the volunteers who continue to give of themselves and work to make our world a better place to live in.

Index